LIFE AND DEATH AT CAPE DISAPPOINTMENT

Becoming a Surfman on the Columbia River Bar

CHRIS D'AMELIO

WITH REID MARUYAMA

LYONS
PRESS

Essex, Connecticut

An imprint of Globe Pequot, the trade division of
The Rowman & Littlefield Publishing Group, Inc.
4501 Forbes Blvd., Ste. 200
Lanham, MD 20706
www.rowman.com

Distributed by NATIONAL BOOK NETWORK

Paperback edition copyright © 2024 by Christopher J. D'Amelio
First Lyons Press edition 2021

British Library Cataloguing in Publication Information available

Library of Congress Cataloging-in-Publication Data

The cloth edition of this book was previously cataloged as follows:

Names: D'Amelio, Christopher J., 1974- author. | Maruyama, Reid, author.
Title: Life and death at Cape Disappointment : becoming a surfman on the Columbia River Bar /
  Christopher J. D'Amelio with Reid Maruyama.
Other titles: Becoming a surfman on the Columbia River Bar
Description: Guilford, Connecticut : Lyons Press, [2021] | Includes index.
Subjects: LCSH: D'Amelio, Christopher J., 1974- | Cape Disappointment Coast Guard Station
  (Wash.)—Biography. | United States. Coast Guard—Search and rescue operations—Pacific
  Coast (U.S.) | Columbia River Bar (Or. and Wash.)—History. | Lifesaving stations—
  Washington (State)—History. | Lifeboat service—United States—Biography. | United States.
  Coast Guard—Biography. | Ilwaco (Wash.)—Biography.
Classification: LCC VK1324.W2 .D36 2021 (print) | LCC VK1324.W2 (ebook) |
DDC 363.28/6092 [B]—dc23
LC record available at https://lccn.loc.gov/2020052928
LC ebook record available at https://lccn.loc.gov/2020052929

ISBN: 978-1-4930-7196-8 (paperback)
ISBN: 978-1-4930-5872-3 (cloth)
ISBN: 978-1-4930-5873-0 (electronic)

♾™ The paper used in this publication meets the minimum requirements of American National
Standard for Information Sciences—Permanence of Paper for Printed Library Materials, ANSI/
NISO Z39.48-1992.

For Courtney, Taylor, Matthew, and Mia

Contents

Introduction by Dr. Dennis L. Noble vii
Prologue by Dave Hofkins. ix

CHAPTER 1: Red Shoes. 1
CHAPTER 2: *Imperium Neptuni Regis*: Crossing the Line. 15
CHAPTER 3: Welcome to Cape Disappointment. 37
CHAPTER 4: Reacting to the Conditions 49
CHAPTER 5: Short Tow, Long Tow. 59
CHAPTER 6: The Graveyard of the Pacific 75
CHAPTER 7: Worst-Case Scenario: The *Linnea* 93
CHAPTER 8: Helmets on Dead Men. 103
CHAPTER 9: "Always Ready". 109
CHAPTER 10: The Peacock Spit Case 123
CHAPTER 11: The Association for Rescue at Sea 143
CHAPTER 12: Last Tow 157
CHAPTER 13: Farewell 169

Epilogue 187
Acknowledgments 189
Index 193

Introduction

Since 1878, a group of people have left the shelter of land and rammed small boats into the angry, cruel sea with a single purpose: to save people from drowning. This group has become part of the US Coast Guard, serving at the USCG's small boat stations. They are aware that they may die in their attempts to save people from the sea.

Yet over the years Americans have not given this group much thought, or even known very much about their work. One of the reasons for this is that few of the men and women have written about just what it is like to live and work at a station, and, indeed, what it takes to push out of shelter on a rescue mission.

Chris D'Amelio has attempted to ameliorate this gap. D'Amelio has held the US Coast Guard's highest level of boatmanship for those who operate the service's rescue boats—that of surfman. The men and women who hold this designation are qualified to take a motor lifeboat and crew out into extremely high seas to bring those in distress back alive.

D'Amelio spent a number of years at the Cape Disappointment Station in Washington, in an area known as "the Graveyard of the Pacific." In this book, he shows us his steady climb to becoming a surfman. "Most Coast Guard stories are grim because they are about life and death," D'Amelio says. "The stories deal with fear, terror, and loss. They remind us of the insignificance of human beings in relation to the sea, and the vast, wild expanses of untamed forces that some venture into. At times they're about true heroism, the kind that takes place every day without an audience or expectation of recognition, the kind we acknowledge only among ourselves."

This book is for anyone who wants to read about man against the sea, to get a glimpse into what the men and women of the US Coast Guard's boat stations accomplish and have to endure. This includes dealing with death, as one part of the work at a station is bringing in those who don't survive. D'Amelio is to be commended for detailing how the work affects the lives of the rescuers' families, who must sit and worry when their loved ones go out into heavy weather. He also illustrates how constant moves can be difficult for the service members' families. Even though D'Amelio made a career of the US Coast Guard, he does not hesitate to question some of the service's policies or some of its leaders.

This easy-to-read and compelling book is one of the better accounts of life at a US Coast Guard station. It will help the general public understand just what happens when the search-and-rescue alarm echoes throughout a station and the crews push out into heavy seas or surf.

—**Dr. Dennis L. Noble,** author of *That Others Might Live: The US Life-Saving Service; The Rescue of the* Gale Runner: *Death, Heroism, and the US Coast Guard,* and *Rescued by the US Coast Guard: Great Acts of Heroism Since 1878.*

Prologue

Thirty-four years ago, I was in seventh grade, dating a girl in eighth grade who had a younger brother. I remember her telling me one day that her brother's sixth-grade class was going to be taking a tour of our junior high school campus for orientation. I was in wood shop when the herd of sixth graders came walking through our class. Among the crowd was my girlfriend's little brother with one of his buddies. Little did I know that these two kids would become my lifelong friends. One of them was Chris D'Amelio.

Chris and I spent years together growing up in our little town of Aptos, California, and most of those years were spent on the ocean. When I close my eyes and think of some of the greatest times in my life, they were with Chris. Surfing. Endless hours spent at Pleasure Point, La Selva Beach, and Big Sur. We would meet after class as often as possible and drive around, hunting waves, eager to get in the water. What a life, I tell myself now.

For me surfing has always been about the fun of it and enjoying the company of good friends. If the conditions weren't good, I'd be happy to move on to something else, like golfing or playing basketball at the park. For Chris, on the other hand, it meant something entirely different. I remember a day that was cold and flat at Manresa State Beach, where I thought to myself, *Okay, time to go home.* The next thing I knew Chris was changing into his wet suit. I said, "I'm not going out there; it's flat and freezing." He said "Okay, cool. Well, you can sit in the car and wait for me."

I did just that. I watched him sit in the ocean just beyond the smaller breaks, staring out to the horizon for an hour and a half, no waves, nothing, just him and the cold gray waters of the Pacific. That more than anything has always defined him in my eyes: Chris needed the ocean. He needed to be in it, and he needed it around him.

Chris has always gone his own way. In this manner, he's always been a leader, showing me by example what independence looks like. I remember when we were still in high school, he would do things that I found strange at the time, and probably were a bit strange for a teenager in general. For instance, he would often go to breakfast by himself and just sit and read the paper. As an adult, it's interesting to look inward and draw out where you learned something that you consider to be a vital part of who you are. But it was instances like this and the time when he just sat in the ocean by himself that taught me you don't need to always be doing something with other people to have a good time. Some things should be just for you, without any need for approval or validation from anyone else.

Chris and I made our way through high school forming a bond that is stronger now than ever, despite the fact that it's been close to three decades since we lived in the same town. It wasn't long after he graduated high school that Chris made the announcement to his family and our circle of friends that he would be leaving and joining the US Coast Guard. Of course, it made perfect sense—Chris doing something that would better his life and create a future for himself. Chris setting off on his own path, following his passion for the ocean.

When Chris left bootcamp I remember how hard it was to watch my brother leave but again, Chris's independence and being the first of us to launch off on his own drove home the lesson of not letting anyone hold you back. Your journey is yours to make.

Once Chris joined the Coast Guard his aptitude and nature helped him to excel. His love for the ocean and his demeanor in chaotic situations are what helped him rise to some of the highest positions in the Coast Guard. If you want to hear stories from a person who has experienced some of the most horrific and harrowing situations imaginable, you have picked up the right book. When I listened to Chris tell these stories, sometimes over the phone the day after they happened, I used to just shake my head in amazement, though what I felt most was pride. Pride that my friend was doing amazing things and truly making a difference in people's lives. You are about to read about the life of a guy who feels more comfortable getting on a boat and driving out into the middle of the ocean in twenty-five-foot seas at two a.m. than going to a cocktail party—a guy whose heart rate goes down when a situation gets more and more intense.

Here's another story that I feel sums up Chris pretty well: He and his team are in the middle of a rescue mission and things are getting pretty hectic: It's pitch black, high seas, people in the water, a boat capsizing—the kind of situation where most of us would be freaking out, shitting ourselves. But Chris, without missing a beat, just leans over to one of his crew and asks him quietly, "So, you interested in going fishing this weekend?" It wasn't that he was taking the situation lightly or that he didn't understand how grave the consequences were. He was simply someone who had mastered the ocean along with his emotions. He was under complete control. That is Chris D'Amelio. That is the friend I grew up with and have come to know so well.

I hope you enjoy this peek into what it's like to be in the US Coast Guard in the Pacific Northwest. Climb aboard, but buckle up. Chris may end up driving you over a thirty-foot wall of water coming straight at you, but don't worry—he's pretty good at it.

—**Dave Hofkins**

CHAPTER ONE

Red Shoes

NEAR 1400 HOURS (2:00 P.M.), MY CREW AND I TOOK THE TWENTY-three-foot utility lifeboat out for patrol. I had two other boat crewmen with me, both fairly new to the station and green, untrained. We were keeping watch on pleasure boats and fishermen around the Columbia River Bar when we got a call from the communications room about an hour later that a boy and girl had fallen off the cliff at the North Head Lighthouse a half mile north of the mouth of the river.

It was the summer of 2004. I was six years into my tour at Station Cape Disappointment in Ilwaco, Washington. I don't remember the specific date—probably because I have chosen not to—and I've never felt the need to go back and find out. I didn't know it then, but this case would be one of the last I would ever work out of Cape Disappointment for the US Coast Guard, and the one that pushed me toward my decision to transfer to Station Siuslaw in Florence, Oregon.

It was late summer, August or early September, near the end of salmon season. Hundreds of recreational salmon boats were out fishing past the Bar, where the water was calm and flat. By noon, the heat had burned off the fog and it was turning out to be a nice day, 70 degrees, not a lot of wind.

The summers in Cape Disappointment, Washington, are traditionally the busiest time of year, especially for the Coast Guard. In the off-season it is a quiet Pacific Coast fishing town, but in summer it becomes a popular tourist destination for vacationers who enjoy the water and want to fish and swim. This makes it the time of year when search-and-rescue stations are most active: Even though the weather is mild, anything can happen when hundreds of pleasure crafts and recreational salmon boats are out on the water, so we perform what is called a Recreational Boating Safety Patrol where we essentially drive around the Bar and up and down and along the coastline, watching, waiting, on standby.

Tourists and visitors are often unaware that the ocean never takes a break, even during nice weather. People underestimate it on beautiful days and are humbled by its immense power on stormy days. Those of us in the Coast Guard see it year-round and learn to respect and cope with its changing personality, from gentle swells to boat-busting breakers. And back in 2004, when the kids fell off the cliff, we Coast Guard officers at Cape Disappointment did our best to help everyone who underestimated the wind, currents, waves, and risks as mundane as slipping off a jetty. We had never considered closing the area to boats when the waves and currents made navigation treacherous; we just did our jobs the best way we knew how.

From the tip of the North Jetty to the tip of the South Jetty, the Columbia River Bar is two miles wide. The station at Cape Disappointment is located on the northern peninsula in Baker Bay, on the Washington side of the river. The station's geographical jurisdiction ranges about fifty miles along the coast, from Ocean Park, Washington, to Tillamook Head, Oregon, and fifty nautical miles out to sea. But when I was on patrol that day, the most significant event I had experienced happened right on the shore, under our noses, and its impact would reverberate through my life for many years afterward.

That day, we took the boat out of the harbor and around the A Jetty. We drove out to the Bar, right along the shoreline, where people were fishing off the rocks. The water was already crowded with boats, kayaks, swimmers, and surfers. Some children on the North Jetty ran after the boat, waving to us as we passed. Even though fishermen tend to have a lot of luck catching salmon here, it can be a very dangerous spot to fish. Walking on the large rocks that make up the jetty, people have been known to slip or get swept out to sea by a large wave. Over my seven years of service at Cape Disappointment, I can recall at least four or five cases where we pulled someone out of the water who had fallen off the North Jetty. At least two were dead bodies. One was a kid.

When we got the call about the boy and girl who'd fallen from the cliff at the lighthouse, we were patrolling a half mile or so from the North Jetty, in the Buoy 10 Fishery, where most of the salmon boats gather in the summer. The watchstander got a phone call from either a park ranger or someone in distress. There wasn't much information to go off of.

"This is UTL five-eight-zero," I said over the radio. "Roger."

"Looks like we got a couple people in the water," Comms said. "Over by the North Head Lighthouse. Over."

"Roger that," I said.

"Looks like two children," Comms said.

We were only about three or four miles away. I told Comms we could be there in five minutes. I turned the boat around and took it north up the coast along Benson Beach. I wasn't worried or panicked. One of the things I've learned over my years in the Coast Guard and being put in difficult situations like this is that when shit does hit the fan, I stay pretty calm. No matter the situation, I can always focus my attention on the task at hand. Still, regardless of the training one has, or the years of experience, nothing is routine when a person is in the water, especially if it's a child. This is one of the worst possible calls to get, one no Coast Guard officer ever wants to receive. Nothing is taken more seriously.

I got into the Coast Guard at the age of nineteen because I grew up around the ocean and was tired of working dead-end jobs. I ended up staying because I was pretty good at it. I discovered I could save lives.

I had first arrived at Station Cape Disappointment six years and eight months earlier, on January 5, 1998. Those who serve in the Coast Guard know the reputation of "Cape D." It is one of the most notorious units in the Coast Guard. The largest station on the Northwest Coast, it has fifty assigned crewmembers who take on more than four hundred search-and-rescue cases every year, more than one a day on average. The station's area of responsibility stretches along fifty miles of coastline, an area often referred to as "the Graveyard of the Pacific" due to the twenty-foot surf, thirty-foot seas, and fifty-knot winds that lead to numerous wrecks every year. More than two thousand vessels and seven hundred lives have been lost near the Columbia Bar alone.

Essentially, Cape Disappointment was where I thought I belonged. During my tenure at Station Cape D, I developed a kind of reputation. I became known as *that guy*—the guy who would go out on search-and-rescue cases when no one else wanted to go, when the weather was extremely hostile, the buoy measuring waves at over thirty feet. By the spring of 2000, I had received my qualification as a coxswain, and fifteen months later, achieved the designation of surfman. By the end of my tenure, I became one of the service's most highly trained and experienced boat handlers.

Becoming a surfman is a rigorous process that takes some people up to four years to complete. Most never make it. Of the 188 boat stations in the Coast Guard, there are only 20 that are located in areas with surf conditions that require surfmen, a qualification more rare than becoming an astronaut.

It is a dangerous job, one that requires finesse and calm in life-or-death situations. The surfman is the guy who drives the boat into twenty-to thirty-foot waves on search-and-rescue missions. He is responsible for the lives of everyone on board, as well as for whatever happens on a case, good or bad. By the time I left Cape Disappointment, I had been involved in over 430 cases and amassed over 2,200 hours of under-way time, operating on the Columbia River Bar. I drove boats into 70 mph winds; I towed fishing boats through storms; I rescued capsized boats from twenty-foot waves. There was nothing else like it for me. I couldn't get enough—the feeling of being out there on a case, in the rough surf, and getting back with everyone safe on board.

Not all cases are dangerous. Sometimes it's the ones that might seem insignificant at first that end up sticking with you the longest. Even though this case of the kids falling from the cliff near the lighthouse was not the most dangerous or life-threatening, it is the one I still think about to this day. I'm sure most people who serve in a branch of the military and see action have a story like this. It is usually a single moment that changes them, for better or worse, even if it's impossible to explain why after years of thinking about it.

The cliff at North Head Lighthouse is about a 130-foot fall with giant boulders at the bottom. The waves pound these rocks in winter and smash boats against the cliffs. There's a reason for the lighthouse's location: The rockbound coastline causes sea conditions that have endangered and wrecked hundreds of marine vessels for centuries, and the torrential force of the Columbia River obscures the view of the lighthouse on the south side of the river, two miles away.

When we got to the scene at the lighthouse that day, I looked around, scanning the water and the cliffs for the kids. I slowed the boat to a crawl. People had gathered up on the cliff near the lighthouse, standing on the railing, looking down at the water. I didn't see a thing at first. Even in the calmest conditions a body in the water can be difficult to spot. I guided the boat slowly along the outskirts of the rocks, keeping a safe distance from the cliffs. Hitting one of these boulders would easily puncture the hull of the boat and capsize it, so I steered carefully around them.

Although I couldn't see anything at first, I knew the kids were there somewhere. I heard them before I saw anything. At the base of the cliffs the girl was caught in an eddy in the rocks, where the water formed a kind of whirlpool. She was splashing and flailing her arms, screaming and crying. I slowed the boat down and got as close as I could without endangering the boat and the lives of myself and my two crewmen. I picked up the radio and let Comms know what I'd seen and what was going on.

"Station Cape Disappointment, this is UTL five-eight-zero," I said. "I have a visual on the girl."

I looked around for the boy but didn't see him.

"Can you get to her?" Comms said.

They had to ask me twice because I didn't hear them. My focus was primarily on how we were going to get the girl out of the water.

The situation didn't look good. She was only about twenty-five yards away but still just out of reach of the boat. There was no way I could get to her. The waves were pushing her under and around in circles, farther and farther away and closer to the cliffs. She was yelling and screaming for help, thrashing at the water. I tried but couldn't get the boat any closer. I looked around again for the boy but didn't see him anywhere. I figured he'd fallen into the water and had already been pulled under the eddy, or else he was caught in the rocks somewhere.

"Five-eight-zero, do you copy?" Comms said again. "Can you get to her? How far away are you?"

"I'm about twenty-five yards away," I said, "but I can't get the boat any closer."

"Can you get to her with a life ring?" Comms said.

I felt my heart beating inside my chest, like a fist pounding its way out, adrenaline reverberating in my bones. Those of us who work in maritime search and rescue know the feeling. There are rarely routine cases, and when children are involved, everyone's heart rate is elevated a couple notches. Even though it takes years of training and qualifications to become a surfman, often in the field you have to be ready to do things you were never trained for—because things so often go wrong.

But that day, nothing went wrong. The conditions were good. There was no fog, so the visibility was fine. There was very little swell, and no wind. Even so, there was simply nothing we could do to combat the situation. It was bad, plain and simple. The waves and current were beating the girl against the rocks at the base of the cliffs. Her body was pinned. She was too far away to throw the life ring, and the twenty-three-foot boat was too large and unwieldy to maneuver through the rocks.

Despite all of these factors, however, I still thought we could pull it off. I thought if one of my crewmen could steer the boat around the rocks I could make a swim for her. We were close enough to hear the waves that were slapping her against the rocks, her bones surely breaking, and I remember thinking that it didn't sound like what I'd imagined.

I turned to my two crewmen.

"Do you think you can drive the boat?"

One said "No," and the other, "I don't know."

I asked them again, not wanting to comprehend the reality.

They said no again.

I wanted to make the swim; I knew I could do it. Every bone in my body wanted to go in after her and pull her out of the water. She was close enough, just twenty-five or thirty yards away, but I couldn't figure out how to do it safely without destroying the boat. We were too close to the cliffs, and I just couldn't put more lives at risk by asking one of my crewmen to take the helm of a boat they didn't know how to drive. I didn't really care about the Coast Guard's rule against leaving the boat; I would have done it if I thought it would have been possible to save her.

All of this meant we would have to leave the girl in the water. It meant we would have to stand there and witness her getting beaten by wave after wave until a helicopter arrived. I knew that the chances of this girl getting rescued alive were slim.

"Five-eight-zero, can you get to her?" Comms said again.

"I think she's too far," I said.

The feeling of helplessness is what I remember most, years later. The children involved were not much older than my own.

"What's the situation now?" Comms said.

I heard helicopter blades coming from the south. The girl's cries for help were getting fainter, silenced by the waves. I stood at the helm of the boat, beating the steering wheel with my fist. I felt helpless and angry. There was nothing I could do—nothing more I could think of to do. I just watched, feeling useless. I watched wave after wave hit this girl and pummel her into the rocks, breaking her bones and filling her lungs with salt water. I watched until the helicopter arrived on scene, the noise of its rotor blades filling my ears.

"We've got a visual on the boy," the pilot said over the radio.

The boy was hanging onto the cliffs. Apparently, he hadn't made it all the way to the water.

"What's his condition?" Comms said.

"He's alive. He looks to be okay," the pilot said.

"Is he in any danger?"

"No," the pilot said.

The helicopter moved closer to the cliffs, getting into position over the girl's body.

"We're going to drop a hook for the girl," the pilot said.

"Roger."

By the time the helicopter had lined up above her, the girl was no longer screaming, no longer moving. Her body was limp, just floating there, getting beaten against the cliffs. I was sure she must be dead, or nearly dead. I was sure that any hope she would make it out alive was probably gone.

The helicopter circled the cliffs several times. I watched it drop slowly, then level off, then lower itself again, more slowly, inch by inch. By now, more people had gathered on the lighthouse cliff and were looking down, shielding their eyes from the sun and the dust kicked up by the chopper. The rotors pressed down, vibrating the air and pulsating against the boat, flattening the waves. It sounded like a thrumming heartbeat heard through a stethoscope, a wall of sound drowning out all other noise. I heard faint voices coming in over the radio, but the sound was muffled and mostly static. I didn't understand anything that was said. Time slowed as I desperately hoped that somehow, the girl might still be alive.

The pilot lowered the helicopter a bit more and held there. The hook and cable were dropped from the cabin of the helicopter, a rescue swimmer coming down on the cable. When the helicopter lifted her out of the water, all I saw were her bright red shoes. It's funny the kind of things you remember. Sometimes I remember only the sound of the helicopter; sometimes, nothing but the girl's screams. Sometimes neither. But I always remember her red shoes.

"We've got the girl," the pilot said.

"What's her status?" I asked.

"She's not breathing. We're going to try to resuscitate her."

I watched the people on the cliff lift their heads as the helicopter rose and the body of the girl was pulled up into the cabin. The water was still. Dust flew everywhere like pollen. Quiet settled around us and in the water. I looked around, realizing we'd been straining to hear the girl's screams above the crashing of waves and pounding of rotor blades, but now it was over. I looked at my two crewmen, their faces a strange combination of shock and childlike disbelief, as if they couldn't or didn't want to believe what had just happened. It had only been about five minutes since we'd arrived on scene, but it felt like hours and hours had passed. In no other case have I ever felt time slow down quite like that, the weight of helplessness pressing against us, pinning our arms to our sides and our feet to the boat's deck. I would think about these five or six minutes for years, replaying the scene over and over, watching it all happen in front of me, powerless. There was nothing I could do.

"That was a mess," one of my crewmen said, breaking the silence.

I didn't know what to say. I don't remember saying anything.

I look back now and tell myself there was nothing we could have done differently. Several people have told me the same thing, and that I shouldn't blame myself. They assure me that I would've only put more lives at risk if I'd made the swim for her. These words never help, though. I have blamed myself for years. I was in charge and therefore responsible; I knew that. That's how it works in the Coast Guard. The fact that my crewmen didn't know how to drive the boat has never freed me from the heavy burden of guilt I feel.

It was a no-win situation where one person has to make the decision to allow another person to die in order to prevent risking three other lives. How does one make that decision? How does someone, willfully or not, let another person die? That was the decision I made that day by not going after her. Was it the right one? I continue to ask myself that question to this day.

The helicopter pilot came over the radio to say he was going to bring the girl back to the helicopter pad at the station after he'd gotten the boy from the cliff. He said a police officer would meet me at the helicopter pad to pick up the boy and contact his parents.

I drove the boat back to the station, unable to think or say anything.

My part of the case wasn't over yet, however. After I'd moored the boat in the dock, the police officer met me at the entrance to the station and we drove to the helicopter pad together. I braced myself to maintain my composure, trying to keep my mind blank as the aircraft landed because I knew what I'd see. This instinctive, self-protective mode might help to prevent long-term impact from an awful situation, but it didn't work this time. As soon as I saw the look on the rescue swimmer's face, I knew the girl was dead.

The girl was still inside the helicopter. She was lying face down with a blanket covering her. I noticed her red shoes poking out from underneath. They were red Converse. I didn't know it then, but I would spend a lot of time thinking about these shoes over the next few years. I could never figure out why they bothered me so much. Now I think it's because they seemed so out of place. They were so ordinary, so happy-go-lucky— shoes anyone could have worn, including my own children.

As the boy got out of the helicopter, the police officer guided him away as the chopper lifted off again to take the girl across the river to a coroner in Astoria.

"What's going on?" the boy asked.

He was about twelve years old, but tall. He was Russian and didn't speak English fluently, so we had some trouble communicating. He kept looking from me to the police officer and then back to me, appearing confused. He seemed to be having trouble understanding what was happening.

The officer turned to me. "I'm not telling him," he said.

What do you say to someone whose sister has just died? I had never given this kind of news to anyone, and didn't want to start today, especially with a twelve-year-old kid.

"Where are they taking my sister?" the boy asked.

It was clear he didn't know the severity of what had just happened. Either he didn't get it or he was in denial, just trying to postpone acknowledging the inevitability of what he'd seen.

"Where is she?" he asked again. "When can I see her?"

My hands were shaking now. I didn't know what to say.

Before this case, I will admit, I had been living high on a fantasy. It wasn't a heroic fantasy, but one probably many service members have had at some point: We all think we are invincible—that nothing can ever touch us. We think that all the violence and death we've seen won't ever get to us. I truly believed that. Before this case, the sight of a dead body had never fazed me. I'd never gone to stress management sessions despite having seen and pulled more than a dozen bodies from the water over the years. I thought nothing bad could ever happen to me.

This would be the first—and last—time I would ever have to give someone information like this, and I felt like crying. There is nothing worse than telling a twelve-year-old child his sister has just died.

"Is she going to be okay?" the boy asked again.

I looked into the boy's face. I thought of my own family—my wife, Courtney, my daughter, Taylor, my son, Matthew. The boy stared back at me without blinking. He seemed to be holding back tears. He seemed to know what I was going to say even before I said it. Maybe he was simply waiting for someone to give him permission to start crying.

"We're going to get you to your parents," I heard myself say. I paused. "Your sister . . . your sister—she didn't make it."

His expression didn't change at first, but then it turned serious all at once. He kept staring at me, and I could see he was beginning to understand. Then he crumpled to the floor. I watched his shoulders heaving, like a painful swell. If he was crying, he was doing it so no one could hear him. The police officer helped the boy to his feet. He was crying less now but speaking in Russian, so I couldn't understand a thing he said anyway.

I followed them to the entrance of the station and watched as the boy got in the backseat of the patrol car. I don't remember if I waved to him or if he waved back, if I gave him any words of comfort. I don't think I did. I just stood there as they drove away, and never saw him again after that.

There would only be a handful or so cases I'd run at Cape Disappointment after this, but nothing like this one—at least, none that I can remember now. Within a month, I would send in a request to my assignment officer for a new unit, and eleven months later I would be transferred to Florence, Oregon, along the Siuslaw River, a few hours south along the coastline. The Coast Guard Station there does not deal with nearly as many cases, and very few as dangerous as those at Cape Disappointment. There, at Station Siuslaw, I would advance to chief, a command position, and would no longer be on the front line in those kinds of situations. I would no longer have to make the call to let one person die in order to protect others. I would no longer drive out into twenty-foot swells to rescue capsized boats, no longer save lives, though I would never really stop thinking about it.

One morning, a couple months into my new tour, I was running along the beach and thought of that Russian boy and his sister. It paralyzed me for a little while. I stopped dead in my tracks and had to sit down and let the feeling of anxiety and grief pass. I would never have guessed then how the memory of that case would live on inside me, casting a shadow over my life. My mind replayed the sounds—the awful feeling of listening to her drowning, the way her screams got quieter as if her voice were an object slowly shrinking until it became the size of a tiny grain of sand as it sank to the bottom of the ocean.

And I would never forget those red shoes.

CHAPTER TWO

Imperium Neptuni Regis:
Crossing the Line

SOME PEOPLE SAY THAT ENLISTING IN ANY BRANCH OF THE SERVICE IS A calling. That wasn't the case for me, but the Coast Guard became my career at the same time I was becoming an adult, a husband, and a father. Certain events motivated me to pursue my enlistment seriously, as a long-term career, rather than it just being a way to make money.

Before I was stationed at Cape Disappointment, I served aboard the 378-foot cutter *Sherman*. I was still finding my way within the Coast Guard, not having any particular goal to achieve during my service.

One day aboard the *Sherman* they were rolling out the helicopter for a disabled boat that had drifted too close to shore. I was taking a nap in the berthing area when I heard it announced over the intercom. The alarm was still blaring, the flight crew still suiting up in the change-out room when I ran up the stairs to the hangar. I was the first one there.

I was part of a four-man tie-down crew whose sole job it was to secure the helicopter when it took off and landed. We were on six- to eight-hour shifts aboard the cutter, which was based out of Alameda, California, and took three-month-long winter trips to Alaska to support the crab fleet in the Bering Sea and along the Aleutian Islands. I was twenty-one, only a year out of boot camp, and had been stationed on board for nearly eleven months. I worked on cleanup details in the mornings and scraped and painted in the afternoon. I was recently married, and this was my third trip to Alaska, my second winter.

The tie-down crew was a four-man team because there were only four tie-down straps. When we moved the helicopter, each person helped tow the straps out to the flight deck, a distance of maybe forty feet. This time I grabbed my strap and started really yanking on it, harder than normal, because there was only one other guy on the opposite side. The flight crew was in the helicopter preparing to take off and the pilot was giving us the thumbs-up, signaling he was ready to go. I put the strap over my shoulder and started really pulling on it, as hard as I could. By then, the rest of the tie-down crew was coming up the stairway. But when I turned around to motion to them, I felt the wheel of the helicopter roll up on my foot from behind. I yelled at them to stop, but it was as if I couldn't hear my own voice. I couldn't hear anything except the heavy drum-like beating of blood inside my skull, pounding in my eardrums, drowning out all other noise.

I felt the bones break in my foot one at a time. Pain shot up my leg instantaneously. When they finally rolled the wheel off, someone cut off my boot and my foot was the size of a football. It was throbbing and felt like it was on fire, radiating heat. It was the worst physical pain I'd ever felt. I was screaming and crying out all forms and variations of expletives, gathering a small crowd, of which I was hardly aware. Soon a medic was on scene, bandaging my foot, asking me about my level of pain and where it hurt the most. Two other crewmen and the medic carried me down to the medical office. By then, the helicopter had taken off.

When the commanders came into the medical office, they were mesmerized by how big my foot had gotten. Captain Roberts was the Commanding Officer, and the Executive Officer was Captain Whitesole, both bureaucrats whose daily rituals appeared to revolve around paperwork and numbers and budget management. I remember they both smelled of aftershave when they walked into the room. Both were really nice guys, as far as bureaucrats go, at least to me and the other crewmen just out of boot camp. They were much harder on the recruits out of the academy. Neither of them had ever seen anything like this before.

"I've never seen a foot that big," said Captain Roberts. "You?"

"Me neither," said Whitesole.

"Looks like you might've broken every bone in your foot."

"What happened?"

"The helicopter rolled over my foot," I said.

"How'd that happen?"

"I don't know exactly," I said.

"This is the plan," Captain Roberts said. "You're going to St. Paul by helicopter, as soon as the helo gets back. From there, you'll get the next flight out to Kodiak. Then Kodiak to San Francisco. Might take a couple weeks for all the flights to come in and fill out all the paperwork, but we'll get you back home," he said. "We'll figure out all the details later. You just get some rest and heal up."

I don't remember having as pleasant an interaction with either of these men in my entire time stationed on board. They were being overly benevolent, almost transparently so. It was obvious they didn't like this any more than I did. Injuries meant paperwork, and paperwork meant someone higher up in the chain of command reading it, which meant questions about mismanagement and proper use of resources. I knew only vaguely how the government worked. They didn't want any complaints or grievances from me; they just wanted the whole thing to go as smoothly as possible, to pass me along through the system as quickly as they could.

"So what do you think?" Whitesole asked. "How does that sound?"

"That sounds good to me," I said. "But do you think I could get something for the pain?"

They gave me some pain pills and I was loaded up like cargo onto the next helicopter leaving for St. Paul, an island in the Bering Sea. It is the largest of the Pribilof Islands, a small chain of four volcanoes. It was also the most depressing and isolated place I had ever been to—vacant and desolate, without a single tree on the whole island, just snow and ice and sea in every direction all the way to the horizon. There was the definite sense of a place forgotten by time, as the town consisted of no more than five hundred people whose livelihood is made possible by the fisheries, by the hundreds of millions of pounds of halibut and cod and crab and salmon shipped to every corner of the globe. Historically the island was home to massive seal colonies hunted by Russian fur traders and the native peoples of the region, the Aleuts, who worked as slave labor, hunting, skinning, and preparing fur seal skins to be sold in Russian markets. Although that was a long time ago, the island still had a small population of native Aleuts when I was there.

The US Coast Guard had a LORAN station on St. Paul, what is often called an isolated duty station. At the time, it was one of twenty-four active stations of its kind that provided long-range radio navigation coverage in areas where the weather was unpredictable and hostile, such as the Bering Sea. It was shut down years ago, but at the time it was manned by a small outpost of about ten crewmen living in one of the most isolated places I could imagine.

The helicopter flew me into the base near dusk and I was wheeled to the sick bay. My foot was X-rayed from several different angles and then

I was taken to a waiting room. The doctor came in and told me I had broken all the bones in my foot leading up to my toes. He said my toes were fine, though, and cracked a thin smile. He told me I wasn't going to like this next thing, but he had to come in every hour or so for the next twenty-four hours to wiggle my foot.

"It's called compartment syndrome," he said, his face turning serious. It meant I had no circulation in my foot. "If it continues, we might have to amputate your foot."

I called my wife Courtney from the phone in the hallway later that night. I told her where I was and what was happening. I told her the plan, repeating what my captain had said almost word for word: I was going to get the next flight out of St. Paul to the station in Kodiak, and then another plane from there to San Francisco.

"It might take a while," I told her.

"Why?" she asked. She didn't understand why they just wouldn't get me down to San Francisco immediately.

The government just works really slow, I told her, which is true. I told her I would call her later and hung up the phone.

I ended up staying in St. Paul for seven more days before they could arrange the next leg of my slow evacuation.

I don't remember much about those days because I was loaded up on huge doses of painkillers for most of the day. I imagine I watched a lot of TV, lay in bed, and tried to learn to get around on the crutches. I remember I was in such a rush to get to St. Paul that I hadn't gotten any of my stuff from the *Sherman*, so I had to borrow clothes. One of the crewmen went into town and got me a toothbrush, some toothpaste, and a razor. I felt like a child asking for these things. To them, I was just something in the way, a body to be moved from one place to the next, like cargo. Unable to fend or care for myself or do much of anything at all, I was of no use to anyone here. I was nothing more than a number and some paperwork to be shuffled, filed, and passed around. By the third day I was ready to leave.

Typically, the base got a flight every five to seven days with supplies and mail. I was meant to be cargo on the next flight going out, but the weather that week was bad. I kept hearing over the radio reports of fishing vessels capsizing, men overboard, people being picked up out of the water. They couldn't land a plane in St. Paul. The runway was frozen over and it snowed sideways all day, and if there were trees, they would have been blown sideways too. It was certainly miserable, and I was glad it was only a stopover for me. A few years later, I remember I heard a story about a man who murdered the station commander over a love triangle, fueled by jealousy and revenge, the news bringing back memories of the island's isolation and barrenness.

The plane finally came in on the eighth day and flew me to Kodiak, which was better than St. Paul, but not by much. There were a lot more people and I was put up in a barracks room, about a two-hundred-yard walk from a bowling alley that had a vending machine that dispensed cans of beer for fifty cents. By then full circulation had returned to my foot and the swelling had gone down, so I could, with some effort, get around on crutches. I ended up spending a few nights at the bowling alley with a couple of the crewmen from the air station, just watching them bowl, drinking fifty-cent beers, joking around, and laughing.

One night, as it got late and I got tired, which is not unusual when mixing pain pills and beer, I decided to walk back to the barracks. Someone asked me if I was okay and I said I was good, I just needed to get some fresh air and rest. We exchanged good-byes and handshakes and I was out the door into the icy streets on my crutches, a pretty good buzz going.

The next morning I awakened sore from head to toe. There were bruises on my arms and legs, and my neck and back were so stiff I could barely move. I called Courtney and told her that it had taken me almost half an hour to get back to the barracks from the bowling alley. Whether it was the wind or the ice or the pain pills or the fifty-cent beers or a combination of all of them, I simply couldn't walk. The crutches kept slipping on the ice and the wind kept pushing me over. My one good leg was wobbly and my head was spinning. I must've eaten shit about seven or eight times, I said.

"You're such a jackass," she said, her usual diagnosis. She asked me how much longer until the next plane left Kodiak.

"Probably another three days," I said.

She sighed with frustration into the phone.

"It's been two weeks already," she said impatiently. "Why isn't someone doing something?"

She still didn't understand, and neither did I, that even though I worked for the armed forces, it didn't mean the government cared about me or would take care of me. I wasn't a priority for them. I tried to reassure her again. I told her I would see her in a few days, which was true. Then I told her that I wasn't going to go out to the bowling alley anymore, which wasn't true. I hung up the phone.

I watched bad TV and ate bad mess-hall food for the next three days before I got on a plane headed for San Francisco. Courtney picked me up from the airport and when I saw her, I realized for the first time how hard these three-month-long trips to Alaska were on both of us, probably more so for her. She had just moved out of her parents' house and into an apartment with me when we'd gotten married a few months before, and now here I was, gone for a third of the year. She wasn't used to being alone so often, and for so long.

We had met a few months after I graduated high school and married three years later when I was twenty-one and she was twenty-five. Twenty-one years later, I sometimes wonder what I ever did to deserve all this. When I look at my wife Courtney and our three children, sometimes I wish I could just sit them down and explain myself to them, tell them about all the things I've seen, all the things I've done; I want to tell them about my life in the Coast Guard, my time at Cape Disappointment.

When Courtney drove us home from the San Francisco airport that day, we knew none of this yet. We didn't know anything about children; we didn't even know a place called Cape Disappointment existed. We were young, without a clue, still figuring it out between ourselves, treading water.

I rested my foot up on the dashboard, closed my eyes, and fell asleep.

Courtney and I met while working at Cole's Barbecue in Aptos. Aptos is a small beach town in Santa Cruz County, right on the northern coast of California where we both grew up and went to high school. It took about five requests from me before she agreed to go out on a date.

I could tell that the age difference bothered her, and I liked teasing her about it.

"Don't you think you're kind of young?" she would ask.

"Come on, age means nothing," I said. "I know a thing or two."

She laughed it off and finally said yes. She was a sweet girl. She knew within a couple of months that she wanted to marry me, though it might have taken me a little longer. We dated for two years. She got a job as a bank teller and I signed up for a couple semesters of fire science and EMT classes at the community college, hoping to either become an EMT or a fireman. Neither happened. When I found out it would probably take ten years to get hired by a fire department, I decided to join the Coast Guard. One day in early January of 1995, my dad drove me down to the recruiter and I enlisted. I was nineteen years old, and had never really left home before.

When I told Courtney I would be leaving for boot camp in a couple of weeks, she wasn't happy about it.

"How long will you be gone?" she asked.

"Boot camp is two months," I said, "but I'll be back after that."

She started bawling and flailing her arms at me, landing punches on my chest and arms. I didn't like seeing her hurt, but there was nothing I could do to console or comfort her.

Joining the Coast Guard wasn't really a new or groundbreaking idea for me. Wearing a uniform was something I'd always imagined when I was a kid. I just didn't know what kind. I wasn't a great student in school and worked hard to get average grades, but I lived for the water. I surfed and swam a lot and spent as much time as I could around the ocean. I even went to Cabrillo College in my hometown of Aptos just to play for the water polo team. That didn't last very long, however, because I wasn't as enthusiastic about my academic studies.

I didn't join the Coast Guard out of any kind of patriotic sense of duty, but it was essential to my idea of success, my sense of self-worth, and my feelings about courage and integrity. I knew I didn't want to join the army, to learn how to kill people. I wanted to serve and help others. I wanted to be respectable, to stand among other respectable men, and to be looked upon as someone who could carry his own weight in the world.

Or at least I believed I wanted all that. I just didn't say any of this out loud because I didn't know how to explain it all to Courtney.

My parents were a different story altogether. They might not have agreed with my decision at the time, but they understood why I thought joining the Coast Guard was a necessary step for me. It didn't matter what I was going through; they supported me no matter what. They have always been like that for as long as I can remember, from the day they adopted me and brought me into their home and family. Both had an extraordinary work ethic and worked extremely hard—my dad for the post office for forty years, and my mom, for the county clerk's office—to get me the things I wanted or needed. When I was six and wanted to surf, my mom signed me up for the Capitola Junior Lifeguards, and my dad bought me my first surfboard and wet suit. It would not be right for me to tell this story without mentioning them. I owe them a tremendous debt, and would not be the man I am today without them. They were the best parents I or anyone could have had. I truly mean that.

The day I left for boot camp my dad drove me to Courtney's house to say good-bye. We hugged and I told her I'd call her when I got there. I didn't cry. I bit my lip and turned and walked away, back to the car where my dad was waiting. The cold wind chapped my face. We didn't say much on the way to the airport. I didn't want to confess to my dad that I was anxious, a bit scared, maybe even numb. I was already being gathered up and numbed by the grip of the current that was taking me far away.

I went through boot camp in Cape May, New Jersey. To get there I took a plane from San Jose to Pittsburgh. I missed my train from Pittsburgh to New Jersey along with three other new trainees, and when we finally got there the drill sergeant chewed us out. He got in our faces and yelled at us, spitting, then had us get on our hands and knees in front of two companies of new recruits and do push-ups for the next five minutes. The message was clear: If you wanted to make it through basic training, you better not be like these guys.

Boot camp was the worst. It was the most miserable two months I've ever known. It was the dead of winter in New Jersey and the streets and sidewalks were covered in black ice in the morning. The wind off the cape was icy and burned our faces when we woke for our five a.m. runs. There was no joy in it, no honor, and very little pride. No respect. It was two straight months of humiliation, of being yelled at, of planks and sit-ups and crawls, push-ups and runs and swims, uniform and bunk inspections, classes and exams, nonstop. Where was the courage? Where was the integrity?

Our company commanders exercised their authority at will and at random. One night at 0200h two company commanders came into our room and threw a trash can. They dumped our footlockers onto the floor, knocked our wall lockers down, tore up our bunks, and ordered us outside into the hallway. It wasn't clear if we were in trouble or if someone had gotten us in trouble or if the commanders simply wanted to remind us of our own powerlessness. We ran and did push-ups and crawls all night. When it was almost dawn, I looked around at the other recruits, panting, breathing hard, trying to catch their breath. The drill sergeant stood us up and said we were going for another two-mile run down the beach before breakfast, and a low groan rippled through the company.

This was the most mentally and physically exhausted most of us had been, or maybe ever would be. The training manual for what we were doing was practically the same one they use in boot camp for the Marine Corps. A lot of us were kids just out of high school who were only beginning to regret whatever impulse had brought us to the recruiter's station a few weeks before, and most were wondering if we had made the biggest mistake of our lives. I was okay. I was hungry, maybe. I was cold and tired and felt my legs wobbling beneath me, my feet weaving in circles as I tried to run. I felt the cold air scraping out the insides of my lungs and slapping me in the face. But I also felt myself transforming into the person I wanted to become.

During boot camp I talked to Courtney as much as possible, which wasn't often—maybe twice a week. Between classes and studying for exams, meals at the mess hall, and training exercises, there just wasn't enough time. When we did talk it was only for five or ten minutes before I had to get off the phone, and we usually didn't say anything of much consequence.

One night toward the end of boot camp, however, I was talking to Courtney on the phone and we decided to get married when I got back.

We had talked about it before but never quite so seriously, and we'd never made any concrete plans. But there was something different in her voice this time. She sounded certain, less victimized and slighted by my absence. This was something she really wanted to do, she kept saying—not because she felt she needed me, but because she believed we truly loved each other. I agreed and hung up the phone.

During the last week of basic training, an assignment officer came in and asked us to put in our dream sheets where we wanted to be placed after boot camp. I told him I wanted to be placed in any unit in Northern California, so I could be closer to home, and that, if possible, I wanted as little as possible to do with law enforcement. I told him I was mainly interested in search and rescue. He told me this really limited my choices as there weren't many units available, but he'd see what he could do. Eventually, I was assigned to the cutter *Sherman*, out of Alameda, California. It was by no means an ideal situation.

I was stationed on board the *Sherman* for two years, one of twelve high-endurance cutters built for the Coast Guard sometime in the 1960s. During the Vietnam War, the *Sherman* had been tasked with supporting Operation Market Time, which involved sorting through hundreds of small vessels in search of weapons smugglers. Thirty years later, while I was stationed on board, we were tasked primarily with supporting the crab fleet, focusing our efforts on search-and-rescue patrols in the Bering Sea and through the Gulf of Alaska, though we also did some law enforcement and drug interdiction along the coast of Central and South America.

While stationed aboard the *Sherman* I traveled all over the world, to places I'd never imagined seeing, like Hawaii and Alaska, Vancouver and Midway Island, to Panama, Colombia, and Ecuador. I crossed over three of the major maritime boundary lines: the International Date Line, the equator, and the Arctic Circle, west and north and far into the Bering Sea, to the very edge of the ice floes, to where you can almost see Russia. The ceremony for such occasions could possibly best be described as an initiation, or a kind of baptism, into the court of King Neptune, with costumes and seawater baptisms. But that was child's play compared to life's real milestones, as I would learn in time.

Three months on a boat is a lot longer than it sounds, and I wasn't quite prepared for the time I would lose from home. Neither was Courtney. Every time she picked me up from the station in Alameda after one of these long trips, it was like we were strangers. The ninety-minute drive back home was always awkward and our conversation was clumsy. It took us a week or so to get comfortable with each other again. I imagine it was hard for her to be in a relationship let alone planning a wedding with someone who was gone for ninety days at a time, then home for thirty, and then gone again.

So while I was home we drank and talked and fought and argued and made up. And we laughed, and when she laughed, she laughed hard, with her entire body. If there was anything I had to offer her at this time, it was that.

Whatever our flaws, we remained the one constant in each other's lives. My job in the Coast Guard has always been difficult on our relationship, even before we were married. When I went into Captain Roberts's office that summer and asked to take leave so I could get married, he told me it wasn't possible because we were heading out for a three-month-long law enforcement patrol to South America. He told me we were going down there to crack down on some drug smugglers. He told me I'd just have to wait to get married when we got back.

Courtney was furious when I told her. She had planned the wedding for that July, and now she was going to have to change all the reservations, cancel the caterer, the photographer, the band, contact all the guests, and then book everything all over again. I hadn't seen her this upset in a while. I reminded her again that I worked for the Coast Guard and sometimes there was nothing you could do. Despite her frustration, she got used to the idea. When she'd calmed down a bit, she said, "Well, I guess that leaves me more time to plan."

The wedding was moved to October. When I got back from the excursion to South America, I got two weeks of paid leave and got hitched.

Before the wedding ceremony, I was drinking beer and shooting pool at a bar down the street with my dad and a few of my childhood friends—Martin Vista, Jeff Wells, and Dave Hofkins, who also happened to be dating Courtney's younger sister, Brooke. It was midafternoon and we had already been drinking for a couple of hours. I was nervous, but ready. We were dressed up in rented suits and tuxedos. We were drunk, but not too drunk. After we left the bar, the rest of the day and the night were a complete blur.

The ceremony was held at a small chapel somewhere in downtown Santa Cruz, not far from the bar. I was self-conscious and cagey and anxious standing up there at the front with everyone focused on me, but all of that went away when I saw Courtney appear at the end of the aisle, framed perfectly by the doorway. The day came into focus, if only for a moment. We stood there holding hands, facing each other, staring into each other's eyes, poised and terrified, terrified but in love, at the edge of a future neither of us could even begin to fathom. We had absolutely no clue, no idea where the tide would take us from here.

The reception was held at the clubhouse of Seascape Golf Course. It was a real party, with close to two hundred people at the reception between my family and Courtney's. There was an open bar and everyone was drinking and dancing and eating, children and grandparents and old and new friends and distant cousins. To this day, I have never seen a celebration quite like this one, with so many people just having a good time, enjoying one another's company. I was amazed by my wife's ability to organize something like this, to plan her dream wedding down to the last detail, and then to just enjoy it, to drink and celebrate, with so many friends and family. The next two decades of our marriage would call upon all of her talents and resources to sustain her and enable her to tolerate all of the absences and the worry, but this was a good start.

The early years of our marriage while I was on the *Sherman* were tumultuous. After I broke my foot, I was assigned to a temporary unit in Monterey. I think it was an adjustment for Courtney, who was used to me being gone so much.

Before the Monterey assignment, Courtney had had to live alone for ninety-nine days at a stretch, working and keeping herself busy. Then I would come home and we would try to adapt to a marriage again, with our husband and wife roles. It wasn't easy, and it often felt like we were starting over every time I came home. Just when we were getting comfortable with each other again, I was off on another three-month tour to Alaska or somewhere else. But I've learned that people can adapt to anything, and perhaps we were getting used to each other's absence.

After I broke my foot, I lived at home and commuted to Monterey for the next four months, the longest I'd stayed in one place since before boot camp. We weren't used to living in such close proximity for so long.

I think it was around this time that Courtney and I first started talking about having children with some seriousness. Or maybe it was the first time the idea was introduced. We were sitting on the couch in the living room, watching TV, when she broached the topic casually, as if talking about the weather or an old memory.

I opened a can of beer and put my foot up on the coffee table. It was still in a cast. Honestly, I didn't think she was ready to start a family. At twenty-five, she was still very sheltered and couldn't handle being alone very well. She still leaned on her parents for support. Not that I thought I was ready either. Nor was it that I didn't want kids. I had always imagined having children, but only after I had established a stable career and believed I could support a family. I reasoned that it wouldn't be fair to Courtney since I was gone so much of the time, and could barely support and take care of the two of us. The timing just wasn't right, I think I told her. We let the topic fall away and our attention was drawn back to the TV. I opened another beer and adjusted my foot on the coffee table.

Over the next several months, the subject of kids ebbed and flowed between us. I could tell Courtney was trying not to bring it up, though it was always there, swimming beneath the surface of every conversation. I felt guilty every time I saw a mother on TV or pushing a stroller down the sidewalk, which was often. When I went to sleep at night, I tried to picture myself as a father, but every time I did I saw myself as if from a distance, lost and wandering in a strange and foreign port halfway across the world.

On my next three-month voyage on the *Sherman*, I told a few other fathers on board that my wife and I had been talking about having a baby, that I was on the fence about the whole thing. None of them were much help. They laughed among themselves as if there were some joke I just didn't know the punch line to. They talked about the diapers, the crying, the year of no sleep. They told me, "Your life is going to completely change." Was that what I feared? Change? Responsibility? I laughed and nodded along with what they were saying, as if I understood the joke. I didn't. Not yet.

When I got back home, Courtney and I had another serious talk. The problem, we discovered, wasn't just my absence. Courtney was mentally and emotionally killing herself. Those were her words. Even her boss and coworkers at the bank were worried about her.

Our relationship changed and we began speaking to each other with sincerity, honesty, and openness. We agreed it was a good thing for her to start seeing a therapist. We also agreed that I would leave my tour on board the *Sherman* and find a new station, one where I could be home more. So the wheels were set in motion. She started seeing a therapist once a week, and two months later I put in for a transfer and was given instructions to report to the Coast Guard cutter *Long Island*, based out of Monterey, at the beginning of the next year, which was six months away. The tours were much shorter, which meant I would be spending less time away from Courtney. It also meant we were going to try to start a family. At the time, I think it was the best thing for our marriage.

Agreeing on these changes allowed us to develop an understanding of each other's needs and desires, our limitations and expectations, and what we were willing to sacrifice for one another. The change was incredible and absolute. Courtney began to grow, becoming stronger and more independent. I saw her put her energy into her work and her home life. She started running, at her therapist's recommendation, and no longer cried when I left. She just hugged me and said good-bye. She didn't have to say anything. I saw it in the way she looked at the babies and the children crying as their fathers got on board the *Sherman*. I could tell she was ready to take the leap.

On my last trip up to Alaska we sailed for three months through the Bering Sea, through the dead of winter. I recall that it seemed like the coldest one I'd been through yet, with fifty-knot winds, and rain and snow and hail. It was during this trip that the *Sherman* didn't make port for more than forty days. The weather was bad and we were the only

Coast Guard resource on this stretch of water, so we had to wait out the storm for additional support to arrive. We waited forty-one days. We ran low on supplies. Provisions were so low we ate chicken and potatoes for every meal. When the ketchup ran out, the crew became cranky and impatient with one another. Arguments broke out for small and petty reasons. Finally, on the morning of the forty-first day, Captain Roberts announced the *Sherman* would be making port in Kodiak.

In port a few of the crewmen took me out to celebrate my last voyage on board. We immediately went from the docks to a bar and nightclub called Mecca, our traditional haunt. I got more drunk that night than I had in a long time. The friends I was with kept buying me drinks and kept getting others to buy me drinks. We laughed and celebrated for no other reason than we were probably never going to see each other again.

At some point someone handed me a can of Copenhagen and I put a pinch of chew into my lower lip and felt the dark ceiling of the room start to spin. The bile of tequila and beer was building up in my throat. I turned around and vomited right on the bar, then I tried to stand up but my legs gave out beneath me. I felt a sudden jerk at the back of my collar and was lifted straight off the ground. By most standards, I'm a pretty tall guy, which means this bouncer must've been the size of a grizzly bear. He lifted me up by my collar and the back of my pants, hauled me to the door, and threw me out. I felt the asphalt rise up to catch me. When I stood up, I puked again and wiped the back of my mouth with my sleeve. I looked around for my friends, or the people I'd come with. They were nowhere in sight. The streets were empty, save for a couple walking down the sidewalk, turning the corner and disappearing down another street. I was alone.

I turned around and started walking back toward the boat, not sure which way it was. I stumbled down the icy streets. My back hurt and my arm hurt and my head hurt. I wondered if fatherhood would be anything like this.

Courtney got pregnant a couple of months into my new tour on board the *Long Island*. It happened almost a year quicker than we were expecting. We found out it was going to be a girl a couple weeks later. Honestly, I was hoping for a boy, but only because I'd heard a girl meant a lot more work, a lot more to worry about. "Worst case for a boy, he goes to jail. Worst case for a girl, she gets pregnant," was the sage advice I'd received from other fathers I talked to.

On the drive home from the ultrasound appointment I ran a stop sign and almost ran a stoplight before Courtney cried out. I'm not sure what I was thinking. Maybe I wasn't thinking. Maybe it was fear or the adrenaline caused by fear. We were stopped at a stoplight when I expressed my concern about having a daughter.

"Then why don't you leave?" Courtney said. "I don't care. I can do it by myself." She was quiet for a moment. I could tell she was joking, but still very serious. Then she said, "Jesus Christ, Chris. You're such a jackass."

I laughed nervously.

"But seriously," I said, "aren't you worried about it, at least a little bit?"

"No," she said. "Not at all."

I couldn't be afraid, not right now, but I was. I was scared shitless. I wanted to help, but it seemed like everything I said or did was like pouring gas on an already burning fire. Over time, I realized it was just nerves talking, and I knew I couldn't let Courtney see that. I had to push it all down—all of my fears and insecurities about being a good father and a good husband—and keep it there, so I could be someone for her to lean on.

I did the best I could. I remember her morning sickness lasted for months, longer than normal. It was the most miserable I'd ever seen her.

The *Long Island* was primarily a law enforcement patrol boat whose area of responsibility ranged all the way up and down the Pacific Coast, and further south off the coast of Mexico. Our trips were a lot shorter than my trips on the *Sherman*, which meant I was home more often. The longest we were gone was for maybe a couple weeks, so I was home a lot of the time during Courtney's pregnancy. After work every day I watched her eat a bowl of cereal, puke, and then lie down on the couch and fall asleep for a couple hours. While she slept, I cleaned. It was like clockwork.

Many people don't know that the US Coast Guard is the nation's leading maritime law enforcement agency. This meant that during my tour on the *Long Island*, we were doing a lot of drug interdiction, although not much of real significance happened to me on board. It was a miserable unit, and I don't miss anything about it. The commander and executive officer were a couple of entrenched bureaucrats with no one's interest in mind but their own. One was a short, thirty-year-old woman straight out of the academy, lieutenant junior grade, who made life pretty miserable for everyone on board. She rode the crew too hard and alienated everyone. Perhaps she was insecure, but she liked to make it known on a daily basis that she was in charge, which put everyone on edge. There was no sense of teamwork or that we were doing anything to help anyone. Mostly we would patrol along the coast of San Diego and Los Angeles and down toward Mexico, boarding small vessels we'd heard were smuggling drugs, though we never found any. I think perhaps we were a useless bunch, not very good at our jobs.

The unit wasn't a good fit for me as I didn't take pleasure in law enforcement. I felt as if my time and skills weren't being used to their potential, but during that year I qualified as boatswain's mate (BM3), a position often considered the most versatile in the Coast Guard. The training for this position included performing all tasks associated with the maintenance of the boat deck, small boat operations, navigation, and supervising personnel. I had also developed a general knowledge of lines and cables and towlines, how to operate cranes and hoists and winches, and how to load and unload cargo and set gangplanks. But mainly I learned how to drive the boats and to use every possible function.

I couldn't stay in Monterey much longer because there were no designated jobs for a boatswain's mate on the *Long Island*, or on any other unit nearby. The promotion to BM3 meant a bump in salary, but mostly I wanted a new unit where I wasn't going to be gone for weeks at a time. Courtney and I decided I should find a unit where I could be home every day, after work. No more living on boats. No more sleeping in bunks. No more eating mess-hall food. No more long trips to distant lands and faraway places.

Without further conversation I sent in my paperwork to my assignment officer requesting a transfer to a station focusing on search and rescue. A couple of days later I received a call from him saying there were three units available, but if I were interested in search and rescue there was a position opening up in the new year at Station Cape Disappointment. That would mean moving to Washington State, he said. I thought he was joking. Cape Disappointment didn't sound like a real place. He assured me it was real and said it was kind of the mecca of search and rescue on the Pacific Coast, the place to test my skills and see plenty of action. Anyone who was anyone in search and rescue at sea had passed through that station at one time or another, he said.

It sounded like the kind of station I wanted to serve at, where I thought my abilities and talents would be put to good use. I told him I had to think about it and talk to my wife, who was six months pregnant. At first Courtney was on the fence about the whole thing, especially leaving her friends and family to move to the tiny town of Ilwaco, but after a week or so she decided it would be good to have a fresh start, in a new place with new people. I put in for the transfer.

Our first daughter Taylor was born at Dominican Hospital in Santa Cruz, California, not long after the New Year, right before I had to report to Station Cape Disappointment. I remember we went on a long five-mile walk along the cliffs in Monterey to induce labor. It was February 12, 1998. It was late in the afternoon when Courtney's water broke. It was nighttime by the time we got her to the hospital. The moon was full, or almost full.

Having a baby was everything that had been advertised and promised: the labor, the screaming, the cries of pain, the pushing, the screaming, and more cries of pain. But then, there was laughter and silence and joy afterward. It was true what I had been told, every bit of it. I had not known joy quite like this before. I remember sitting in the chair holding my newborn daughter Taylor for what must have been hours, though it felt like minutes, with my wife Courtney in the hospital bed next to me. Both were sleeping and the silence was so absolute. The hours slipped by until it was nearly dawn and I heard the world awakening. Not long after that day, I had to report to the station at Cape Disappointment when the baby was only two weeks old, so I left for Ilwaco, Washington, leaving Courtney behind.

Each morning in Ilwaco began with running up the rocky cliffs through the fog and into the woods overlooking the Bar and mouth of the Columbia River, my way of preparing for the day, mentally and physically, and of making the transition from home to work. Getting to know the landscape was a vital part of my education at Cape Disappointment. It's where I would study and learn everything I could about the way the water behaves, including tides, currents, waves, and the shifting sands beneath what's widely considered the most dangerous bar entrance on the Pacific Coast. When I first moved there, it was raining and there was always wind. Our first year there was an unusually bad period for the Pacific weather phenomenon known as El Niño, and it seemed like it rained seven months straight.

A couple days after I arrived I woke up earlier than usual one morning and ran the trails behind the station. I followed the contours of the cliffs, the air full of moisture from the ocean and the sharp scent of spruce. The air was cold and gray and an early wind whipped through the tops of the trees, the waves pounding the cliffs below. The tide was incoming, with a twenty-foot swell, and the wind feathering the tops of waves, whitecapping. I ran hard, until I felt my legs and hands trembling. In a couple days Courtney would fly up to Ilwaco with our newborn daughter, leaving behind everyone she'd ever known, her family and her friends and her coworkers, for the first time in her life and move to a small town where she knew no one. Together, we would stand at the edge of these dark, violent waters, with no one but each other.

CHAPTER THREE

Welcome to Cape Disappointment

Ilwaco, Washington, was a small fishing town with a population of no more than nine hundred people when we lived there, from January of 1998 to June of 2005. There was one fast-food restaurant, one small grocery, and a couple of bars. Liquor stores sold firewood and fishing bait.

Courtney and I didn't know a single person when we arrived, and other than going to work or the grocery store, I don't think either of us left the house for the first couple of weeks. It was a difficult adjustment for Courtney, who had never really been outside our hometown before. Now with a newborn baby to care for, we really were on our own. Or rather, Courtney was on her own. I worked a duty schedule of two days on, two days off, so I was home half the time, leaving Courtney alone half the time. Those first few weeks I remember Courtney crying a lot and the baby crying a lot, and feeling helpless to stop their sorrow.

On my first day on duty I was taken up to the watchtower cliff overlooking the Columbia Bar. The watchtower had a full view of the North Jetty and Peacock Spit, with close to a 360-degree view of the surrounding area. To the east and down the cliff were the station and mess hall and the boathouse docks. To the north, the gym and maintenance house, the communications room, and the barracks beyond them. To the west and south was nothing but ocean and the hazards of the Columbia Bar.

It was the middle of winter and there were twenty-foot waves rolling in off the sandbar, pounding the entrance of the river. There was a thick fog bank standing a few miles offshore, and heavy wind. It was raining steadily. The watchstander was young, in his late twenties, not much older than I was. He received a call from the Bar boat and reported it to Comms. Every morning, the Bar boat does a routine patrol checking the conditions in four spots on the Columbia River Bar: the middle grounds, Clatsop Spit, Peacock Spit, and the main channel. Several bathymetric charts covered the far wall and a pair of heavy-duty binoculars stood at the center of the room. He leaned over the desk and made some notations on a report sheet, observing the weather conditions, making note of the wind speed and the direction of the swell every thirty minutes, noting changes.

The Columbia River Bar is temperamental and unpredictable, even volatile. Even the most experienced boat operators have a hard time guessing what it could do from one moment to the next. What makes it so dangerous and unpredictable is the constantly shifting sandbar, as well as the fact that, unlike other major rivers, the Columbia doesn't have the benefit of a delta or a slough. Here, the two-mile-wide river shoots directly into the oncoming waves of the Pacific, and conditions can change from calm to life-threatening within moments, due to shifts in the direction of wind and swell.

Far below, I could hear the waves striking the bottom of the cliff and felt the rumble vibrate through my legs, like music. I looked west out past the A Jetty, marveling at it. I'd never seen such waters before. I was seeing it for the first time, realizing its dangerous potential, how forbiddingly powerful and unpredictable it could be, and within five minutes I knew this was where I belonged. I had always been drawn to extreme conditions like these, maybe to learn what the sea is capable of. I grew up in and around the ocean my whole life, surfing and swimming, and I wasn't frightened by it. I knew how to read it and believed I could get the better of it, or learn to. I was young and arrogant and believed I was untouchable. Believing that was my first step in a dangerous direction.

"Welcome to Station Cape Disappointment," the watchstander said.

"Thanks," I said, not taking my eyes off the pounding surf.

My training to become a surfman started almost as soon as I arrived. Cape Disappointment is also home to the National Motor Lifeboat School, the only school for rough weather and surf rescue operation in the United States. It is where most of the great and legendary heavy-weather surfmen are trained.

Originally, surfmen had a nominal role in the Coast Guard. Historically, they were required to walk the beaches along the eastern coasts in an effort to discover distress situations. Once each surfman reached the end of his patrol zone, he met the surfman of the next zone and they exchanged checks, to prove that each had covered his intended search area.

Nowadays, the surfman is a mainstay in search and rescue at sea. They perform all major functions of commanding a crew and driving and operating boats in heavy surf conditions. The process of becoming a surfman is rigorous and takes some four to five years to complete; most never make it. The skills required include mastering communications and navigation; all the duties performed by the crewman and the coxswain; and then, finally, qualification as a surfman by testing. It is one of the most dangerous jobs in the Coast Guard, and the most difficult to qualify for. Only a small percentage of eligible coxswains make their surf qualifications, something like 10 percent, and there have only been five hundred or so qualified surfmen in the history of the US Coast Guard. The first surfman to be qualified was in 1871. It takes a certain kind of temperament, the right demeanor, which not everyone has. From the time I became a coxswain to the time I became a surfman, it took me a year and three months to complete all of the qualifications.

Cape Disappointment was known for producing some of the most skilled boat handlers. Many surfmen after retiring from the Coast Guard found civilian work as bar pilots or pilots for deep draft boats, the same way pilots in the Air Force work for airlines after they retire. Others become teachers and trainers.

One of them was a man named Kyle Hoag. He was a teacher at the Motor Lifeboat School before coming to Station Cape Disappointment as an Executive Officer (XO). Although he was well-known and respected among the surf community and very knowledgeable, he wasn't well liked at the station. He had worked at Station Siuslaw and Station Umpqua on the Oregon coast, and had been influential in the training of many successful boat drivers, including the second woman ever to be qualified as a surfman. He had been around the surf community for a long time and knew what he was talking about. I was never sure if he liked me much, and I know he was leery of me. He probably thought I was young and impulsive and arrogant, and I don't think he trusted me, at least early on, to make difficult decisions. But over time what started out as friction between us became respect.

I knew the behavior and patterns of the ocean better than most. Growing up in Aptos, right on the water—including swimming and surfing in ten- to fifteen-foot breaks—gave me an edge. I had learned to read the waters at a young age, and so handling a boat in such conditions was very natural for me. I knew pretty early on I was good at reading the ocean: wave speed, wave direction, when they were going to break, where they were going to break, how many were in a set, and the timing of the set.

By the time I was crewman-qualified I had to know all the specs, the limitations, and the draft length on all the boats, of which there were five: a fifty-two-foot Triumph, a twenty-three-foot utility boat, a forty-four-foot motor lifeboat, and two forty-seven-foot motor lifeboats. I had to learn the electrical components of each boat, to familiarize myself with the engine, the break room, and the machinery. I had to learn each boat's characteristics to determine which was best suited for certain kinds of tasks, or certain kinds of weather.

We did most of our surf training in the forty-seven-footers. They were newer boats, designed to roll over waves rather than crash right through them, which means learning to drive one of these boats requires just as much finesse as it does guts. Hands are always on the throttle, feathering; small, subtle movements are best, not all-ahead or -astern. A surfman is always measuring the waves and knows when to hammer down on the engines and when to ease off. Knowing how to hold a boat steady in storms was everything.

Close calls at Cape Disappointment happened all the time. It was a fact of life here, a fact you had to live with on a daily basis and be able to react accordingly. It didn't matter what the weather was like because anything could happen, at any time. In the summer of 2001 I had just returned to Ilwaco from a thirty-day leave in Aptos while Courtney and Taylor stayed behind for a couple days with her mom and dad. I was sitting in my truck early one morning at Waikiki Beach, just around the corner from the Cape D station, watching the waves. They were coming up over the North Jetty, making the rocks slick.

Suddenly a head popped up over the jetty behind the drift and giant boulders. It was a man, waving frantically at me. I got out of my truck and climbed over and through the jetty as the sound of a woman screaming got louder. She had snapped her leg, a compound fracture and a dislocated ankle. The man said it happened while walking on the jagged rocks when a large piece of drift rolled over her leg. Her ankle was bent so far backward that her leg looked like three sides of a square. We carried her back to the parking lot and put her in my truck. She screamed the whole way to the hospital. I blew through a stoplight and told the couple they would have to cover my ticket, trying to lighten the mood. When we got to the hospital, they flew her off to Portland and I never saw them again.

One of my first lessons was that something was always happening at Cape Disappointment, that it often tended to get out of control. That's what happened a couple of months before I got qualified when our training officer wanted us to go out and mess around on the 47s. We were in the surf about an hour and the waves were about eight to ten feet, nothing too big or crazy or unmanageable, but then we started hunting for waves, looking for trouble. When people do that, things tend to go bad.

As the other boat was lateraling into the surf zone from Buoy 10, they got caught in a set of waves. It wasn't completely unusual for this to happen; their timing was just bad. When the swell is eight to ten feet, you can still get an occasional thirteen- to fifteen-foot set of waves, and their boat got hit with one of those. Our boat was already in the surf zone. We watched as the wave hit them on the starboard bow section of their boat, which did a reverse pitchpole, capsizing end to end. They rolled from bow to stern, which isn't normal. They went under, immediately, and were completely upside down, so all we could see was the bottom of the boat. None of us knew what to do.

Four of our coworkers, all colleagues and friends, were on that boat, we realized, holding our breath. Everything is going to be okay, was all we were thinking. Everyone on the boat was clipped into surf belts, so no one was going overboard or would be sucked out to sea, but the boat was turned over for what seemed like a long time, and I could tell our training officer was beginning to worry. When the boat finally righted itself and turned back over there was a loud clang of metal and all the alarms were blaring. The engine room was flooded and one of the windows had been smashed out. Everyone was alive, but banged up pretty bad. We escorted them out of the surf zone and back to the station, where an emergency medical crew was waiting. Someone ended up with a sprained wrist, someone else, with a concussion. Other than that, the looks on their faces said it all. I could see the excitement had vanished from their eyes. They looked scared, shaken up.

Some might call this job bravery; others might call it stupidity. I say it's a complicated combination of both. But there's a difference between putting your body in harm's way to save another's life and putting your body in harm's way because you enjoy it. For a while I mistook one for the other. I enjoyed that feeling of adrenaline. I reveled in the feeling of a racing heart. I was hooked on it. Being in the Coast Guard was a way to make a living while frequently enjoying those surges of high-octane adrenaline, then wrapping up the shift with a feeling of satisfaction that I'd challenged the ocean, read the conditions right, and got back home intact. It was an extension of my childhood, really.

I grew up on the beach, surfing. I started when I was eight years old. By the time I was in high school, I had surfed every break in Santa Cruz County with my old friends, Jeff Wells, Charles Kenyon, and Dave Hofkins. Once we could drive, we surfed further south into Monterey and north up the Pacific Highway, into Davenport and Half Moon Bay. Compared to Santa Cruz, Ilwaco had very little in terms of good spots. There were big waves, but there weren't many places you could paddle out. If you wanted to surf, you had to work for it, and paddling out was never easy.

Every morning I had duty at Cape Disappointment I woke up early, well before my shift began, usually when it was still dark out. I ran five miles, then sat on the A Jetty for ten or fifteen minutes and watched hundreds of good-looking waves go through there, perfect left-to-right breaks. I spent a good amount of time sizing it up, trying to figure out the best way to get out there. In several months of close observation I never saw a single person paddle out, and figured either no one surfed here, no one saw the potential to surf here, or everyone was just too scared to even try. I concluded that people must have been aware of the reputation this place had and knew it was best to be cautious.

But my own private spot, the A Jetty, was fairly secluded, located on base just south of the Motor Lifeboat School. The water was a mix of incoming tide from the ocean and outgoing tide from the Columbia, and the waves were always good. One morning I decided to paddle out alone. There were long period swells, eight to ten feet, with sets of three waves coming in, crashing on the sandbar. It was about as misguided a thing as I'd ever done before. I was off duty and there was no one there to spot me, no one to call 911 if anything happened.

One of the dangers of surfing the A Jetty was the shipwreck of the *Bettie M*, a tuna boat that ran aground in 1976 directly beneath the Cape Disappointment Lighthouse inside the mouth of the river. A missed wave or a poorly timed dive could leave you mangled in the wreckage. Then there was the problem of navigating the long bed of razor-sharp rocks on the beach, continuously thrashed and pounded by the waves.

I didn't make it very far. The swell wasn't manageable. A large outside set came in as I was still paddling out and within moments it became evident that I wasn't going to make it over the waves. I tried to dive under the first wave. It didn't work. The white water pushed me down and I felt myself hit bottom immediately. I tried to swim up but another wave came crashing down on me, and I felt myself pulled down hard by my board. Then another wave came. And another. Each wave was a ten-pound sledgehammer striking the top of my skull. My ears were ringing. Black spots flowered at the center of my vision. I swam to the surface but was plunged back down again. I lost all sense of direction. Up, down, left, right. I tried to swim up again but couldn't move. I was pinned to the bottom.

For a moment I thought I was going to die, right there. It was the first time this thought had ever crossed my mind, but definitely not the last. This is it, I remember thinking; I was practically certain of it. It felt like I'd been under for five or ten or fifteen minutes already, struggling to get to the surface, but the more I tried, the worse it seemed to get, like quicksand. First there was fear, then came sorrow. I felt myself inhaling huge gulps of water. I thought about my parents, my friends. I thought about Courtney and our daughter Taylor. They were at home right now, sleeping or eating breakfast. I thought about the night we got married, about the night after Taylor was born and I held her, asleep in my arms, all night. I thought about not having them anymore, about them not having me.

Then the waves just stopped coming. I had been dragged in a good seventy-five yards and was no longer taking the waves right on top of me. I felt myself floating there, suspended in the water, as if a fifty-pound weight had been lifted off my head, and I made a last surge up to the surface. I had to time my exit between a series of smaller waves, trying to avoid getting plastered against the rocks. When I got out I crawled up onto the rocks and puked up gray water. I was seeing black spots at the edge of my vision. I threw up more water. I lay on my back and tried to breathe. When I got back to my truck I sat there for about ten minutes, just staring at the windshield.

"You okay?" I heard a voice behind me.

A guy in a park ranger uniform was standing on the jetty above me. I'd find out later his name was Scott. We would become good friends and surf buddies over the next few years.

"You were out there for like ten or fifteen minutes," he said. "You sure you're good?"

I nodded my head.

"I wasn't sure if I should call someone or go out and look for you," he said.

I clenched and unclenched my fists.

"Man," he said, "I thought you were really dead."

We shook hands and introduced ourselves. I felt the adrenaline, the pulsing of blood inside my skull. Truthfully, I was scared and felt like I needed to puke more. The certainty of death was never what frightened me. I think I was frightened more so by its daily presence, its unceasing possibility. This incident made me realize that at any time, at any moment of chance or fate or bad luck or just plain stupidity, I could be snuffed out. Simple as that, and without any warning signs. There would be no rays of light, no light at the end of the tunnel. My life would not flash before my eyes. It would be swift and all of a sudden, then gone.

Most of the training to become a surfman is spent on a boat, under way, driving in breaking surf and in breaking bar conditions while simultaneously performing practical exercises. Training exercises like putting a boat in tow, dewatering a boat, passing a pump, or picking someone up in the water are the basic tasks that must be performed in varying weather conditions, and with a certain calmness of demeanor, to even be considered as a surfman. Then, after all the qualifications and training, you have to pass an oral review board.

I passed my oral review board on October 30, 2000, after failing the first time. The first time I'd stood in front of four of the most qualified boat drivers at the station and the Motor Lifeboat School. Our XO was an old-school boat driver named Dan Burkes, and like most of these old-school guys, he believed the new generation of search-and-rescuers was growing soft. He believed that if you couldn't tow a boat in fifteen-foot waves, you shouldn't be qualified. He believed if you second-guessed yourself or had a hard time making difficult decisions, you shouldn't be qualified.

The first time I stood in front of this group they took turns asking me questions and I stumbled over my answers for an hour. It felt like days. I couldn't find the proper wording. Most of what they asked were typical situational questions, such as, "How do you perform a slip tow?" or "How do you tow a boat through the Bar?" or "If a body is in the surf zone, how would you get them out?" or "If a boat is taking on water in ten-foot surf, how would you approach them and what measures would you take to both ensure the safety of your crew as well as the passengers on board?"

Some of their questions were more ruthless; others were critically important; and some were simply meant to fluster me. I could tell they were preying on my nerves. When I lost my use of words, I tried to make a diagram of my answers on a whiteboard, but found I was having a hard time remembering the buoy numbers.

"Why is the green buoy purple?" asked Kyle Hoag.

I was trying to show the path that I would take while towing a boat, to get them safely back to the channel, but in the diagram on the whiteboard I had labeled all of the green buoys purple. There was no such thing as a purple buoy, only red and green buoys, which are used to guide boats coming in and out of the Bar. The red buoys you kept on your right coming back in, the green buoys, on your left. At first, I didn't know what to say and felt my face burn red.

"I only had a purple marker," I said.

He wrote something down on a piece of paper.

"Okay," he said. "Thank you. That'll be all."

I left the room feeling small and defeated. I stood in the hallway and listened to them talking inside. When they called me back in, they told me in a few words that I didn't pass, and it wasn't a big surprise. I had let myself get rattled. I had allowed the fear of failure to overwhelm me.

The second time I was in front of the oral review board, I passed. This time I brought the right-color markers and answered the questions simply and to the point. Once I was qualified and given my surfman pin and certificate, Kyle Hoag pulled me aside in the hallway to congratulate me. We shook hands. I thanked him. He told me he was sorry for giving me a hard time at my first review board. By asking those questions the first time, he said, he'd just been trying to rattle my cage, to push me. "When you're out there in the surf you have to be familiar with that feeling of panic," he said. "Every night when you have duty, or when you're just lying in bed, think up different scenarios, different situations. Try imagining the worst thing that can happen, and then the worst thing that can happen after that. And try to imagine how you will respond."

It was some of the best advice I ever got from anyone, and I know I was better for it. Over the years it kept me mentally prepared, made me better at my job, quicker with my decisions, and more resolute.

However, in other ways it kept me away from home. The ocean and its currents were already beginning to consume me.

CHAPTER FOUR

Reacting to the Conditions

IT WAS ALWAYS RAINING IN ILWACO, MAYBE TWO-THIRDS OF THE YEAR, sometimes more. I know the rain got to some people, and Courtney was among them, but it never bothered me much. I was drawn to the bad weather and the extreme conditions, which unfortunately led to the dead bodies and gave this place its nickname, "the Graveyard of the Pacific."

The dead bodies we pulled out of the water fit several categories. Many were fishermen who had washed overboard, or someone who had slipped off a jetty and was swept out to sea. Others were suicides, which were not uncommon. I think the weather got to most people around here, especially in the winter, when the sun vanished for weeks or months on end, leaving a colorless fog hanging in the sky. The waves struck the cliffs and the wind whined through the clifftop trees and the rain beat down. If you didn't know any better, or if you were superstitious, you'd think there was something cursed about this place.

In my second winter at the station I was just beginning to break in as coxswain, working in the deck department, maintaining the boats and all the equipment on them. During the day four of us worked on the boats until lunch, after which we would get under way for training. In the evenings we were on standby, so we played volleyball or basketball or fished off the jetty.

One typical winter night in the Pacific Northwest, gloomy, drizzly, and cold, I pulled duty and was working in the watchtower. Around 2100h, the watchstander piped the first boat crew to the fifty-two-foot Triumph for an escort. There was some swell, but nothing huge. It was nothing to worry about.

The coxswain was Bill Brewer, who was from Hawaii. I met him at the locker room, with a mechanic and two other crewmen, and he told us to change into our dry suits quickly. We were under way within three minutes. Bill Brewer was old school in that he didn't talk much, but I could tell by his silence that whatever we were going to was bad. The boat that needed help was a fishing vessel, a crab boat, about a half-mile outside of the Bar. When we got within a hundred yards of it Bill gathered us together at the helm and told us the situation. He was serious, all business.

"One of the crewmen got his head stuck in the block," he said, pausing long enough for the information to sink in. A block is a winch that is used to haul in crab pots. Bill looked at each of us, as if to remind us of the seriousness of our job. "Decapitated," he added.

As we approached the fishing vessel, Bill made contact with the captain via radio. He reminded us again to keep calm, because no one on the crab boat was going to be, and it was our job to handle the situation like professionals.

"If you need to puke," he said, "do it where no one can see."

We escorted them back to the boat basin in Warrenton, between Astoria and Seaside, a twenty-minute drive. When we got within a hundred yards of the pier, I saw a huge crowd of people waiting there—family, friends, police officers, an ambulance, a fire engine, and news reporters.

Bill moored the boat and the fishing vessel was docked. A police officer boarded and walked around the boat. He picked up the head and walked it over to where the body was lying at the stern while everyone on the dock watched. My stomach churned—not just because of the sight of such a thing, but because I knew what was happening to the family and friends standing on the docks. The expressions on their faces changed instantly; any hope they had evaporated, and their despair became visible and audible.

I looked over at Bill and his expression was livid, his face a white mask, the tendons standing out on his neck. This was always the worst part of the job, the most difficult for me. I never got used to seeing people hurt like this, watching them crumble to the ground, their lives shattering in a moment. Part of the responsibility of my job, I learned, was to help ease this mortal pain, to soften the blow. The police officer might not have known what he was doing at the time, but what he did had consequences for these people's lives. I'm sure they never forgot this moment. I'm sure because I never did.

I couldn't talk about events like these, or bring them home with me, so I internalized them. As a result, even when I was at home, I was never really at home, especially in my early years working at Cape Disappointment. It took years of witnessing such pain and anguish to learn how to balance the violence and cruelty and indifference of my work with the calm and peace and stillness of home life. And because we lived so close to the station, at first it was difficult for me to separate between the two.

When Taylor was born, Courtney's energy was focused solely on her. For a couple weeks, she barely went past the front door. She worked at setting up the baby's room and decorating and arranging the house, the beginnings of our first real home: the furniture, the kitchenware, the hand towels and bath towels, the drapes, and the pictures and the picture frames. Courtney has always been that way. When she does something, even the smallest task, she has to focus on it 100 percent. It's hard for her to multitask or divide her attention in any way. I guess we're similar in that regard.

By the time we were settled in at our new home, I felt useless, like a third wheel. Courtney and Taylor had their own routines, rituals, and daily activities that I was not a part of. I had been told that in the first couple years of a baby's life they need their mother more than their father, which made logical sense. Although I still wanted to be of use, I didn't quite know how, which made me constantly doubt my ability to raise a child. Most of our friends were single and not many had children. We had no one to talk to about it except our own parents, so we had no local models of how people dealt with kids. I knew that fatherhood demanded a drastic change, the embrace of responsibility and an obligation to protect and care, but unlike handling a boat I had little innate knowledge of raising children, so I groped around for cues and hoped to stumble into a useful role.

What I did know was the ocean and how to drive boats. It's probably one of the few things I've managed to truly master in my lifetime. Part of the reason I became such a good boat driver was because I had an innate sense of the way the ocean works from spending my childhood in and around it. The other part was because I was eager and wanted to learn firsthand. I spent as much time as I could out on the water, on the boats, on search-and-rescue cases.

Courtney and I lived in a small house not far from the station. We were close enough so I could hear when the SAR alarm went off, and half the time I was the first one down at the boat docks or the communications room, volunteering to go out. By the time I was a year into my training, I had almost twice as much under-way time as some of my peers, which was part of the reason I qualified for surfman so quickly, after two years.

There's a lot to think about when driving a boat through rough surf, a lot that can go wrong. If you lose an engine, hit the bottom, if you're not square, roll the boat, or capsize, you must be ready to react. And if you mix all those possibilities with trying to rescue a boat in distress or picking up people in the water, there's a lot more you have to consider, and a lot of split-second decisions you have to make, with no time to second-guess yourself. In heavy surf, hindsight is not really a luxury you can afford.

After I made the first-class rank, I began teaching and training the incoming and break-in surfmen. I'd been working at Station Cape Disappointment for four years and had a reputation. I liked to push the envelope. I liked to take risks that others weren't willing to take.

For instance, I liked to train the new crewmen in the big stuff, when the swell was over the training limitations of fifteen feet. Depending on where you measured the wave from, however, it meant we could get up to eighteen-foot breaks. I believed in Kyle Hoag's school of thought: Teach and train the next generation of search-and-rescuers to be better than you were. I believed training the new crewmen in the real big stuff was the best way to prepare them. Most of the time it was pretty routine; standard procedure was to lateral in, square the boat, take a few breaks, and lateral out.

"Try to be as smooth as possible," I said a lot. "Don't ride the engines, feather the throttles." But of course, that standard instruction was subject to the conditions.

One time, I was doing a check ride for one of the break-in surfmen whose name was Mike Sanders. The check ride was the last qualification, the final under-way time before he had to pass the oral review board. These were supposed to be routine—just a simple drive out into the surf zone, usually Clatsop Spit, and back—but I decided we would go to Peacock Spit. Mike was competent. I knew he could drive a boat, so I thought it was important to make his check ride a real test. This was his last step before his oral test for surfman qualification, and as such, more important. Another lifeboat followed us on the way out.

Peacock Spit, just outside the Bar, never looks as big as it actually is. I never figured out whether it was the reflection of the rocks on the bottom or the way the light hits off the water that fooled us into thinking the surf there was manageable. Once we got close, into the surf zone, I realized it was way too big and started thinking about getting out. I radioed to the second boat to stand by, to not follow us, but they didn't need to be told. They'd already decided to hang back once they'd seen the surf we were in.

We took four or five big breaks, the waves crashing directly into the bow and spraying whitewash twenty feet into the air, like a whale spout. The entire boat shook. Then the rain started pounding on us, reducing visibility and adding to the challenge. About ten minutes passed before I decided we should call it quits because the surf was way too big for any kind of significant training. That's when we discovered we couldn't make a move or lateral out of the surf zone because the wave sets just kept coming and coming, one after the other, like a freight train. At that point, we were strictly in survival mode.

We were on the water for close to an hour, getting hit from every direction: eighteen-foot breaks, thirty-knot winds, rain that stung like BBs. My bones were hurting, my arms and legs were sore. Mike had to be sore too, but it wasn't something we chatted about. We were focused on reacting to the conditions, keeping the 47 pointed into the oncoming waves. He probably learned more than he bargained for that day.

One of the dangers of being in a surf zone is the concentration of oxygen in breaking waves: The frothy spume on the surface that the boat rides in becomes light water that the props can't bite into, stealing power from the engines. You can have the throttles pushed to the limit, full ahead, and only get a fraction of the speed and control you normally would. The forty-seven-foot lifeboat had 435 horsepower and could go 30 kilometers per hour on flat water, but in surf conditions it's usually necessary to hold back or the boat could reverse-pitchpole, flipping end over end.

After an hour I figured the swell would let up soon, but it didn't. We were stuck in the surf zone, watching as an outside set of four to five twenty-foot waves was lining up, gathering power, moving menacingly toward us. I told Mike he had to hammer down the boat engines and he looked at me like I was insane. I usually trained my boat drivers to be as smooth as possible with the boat, to ease it through the surf zone. He knew that going full speed into a wave this big could do some serious damage to the boat, as well as to us. But I knew waves this big could wash the boat onto the beach or capsize us—or worse, shatter us against the rocks.

Mike punched the engines, taking us up from seven to ten knots. We hit one wave head-on and it felt like running at full sprint straight into a concrete wall. The boat backed up a hundred yards. I held on as my body jerked right, left, up, and down with the turbulence. We hit another one and backed up another hundred yards. There was another, then another. They just kept coming and we couldn't move. In all the scenarios I'd run through my head, this had never been one of them, and I didn't have a plan.

"Just be patient," I yelled to Mike over the roar of the wind and waves. "We'll find an opening."

Mike's demeanor was calm, but I could tell by his face that he was worried, or maybe freaked out is more accurate. He knew we were just trying to survive. Being a trainee wasn't any guarantee he'd walk away from this because this wasn't a fake situation that he could tap out of. It was hairy. The waves kept pushing us closer and closer to the shore and the rocks. I told him to just keep the throttle down. I knew there wasn't much else we could do but wait it out, keeping as much distance as we could from the cliffs. I reminded him once more to just keep the throttle down, knowing that flinching or backing off even for a second could be deadly.

I was nervous but I never showed it. I realized it had been a mistake taking a trainee out on the water when it was like this, but I'd done it anyway. In the back of my mind I knew I should take over the controls just to get us out of there, but I didn't. I rationalized that if he passed his exams based on a mundane check ride to Clatsop and made surfman, he might find himself out in these conditions without someone more experienced to back him up.

If anything happened to either of us, it would be on me. I knew if I could just manage this, if I could get us out of this mess, I could take care of the next thing and then the next thing. That was the simple, secret key I'd learned. Over the years I developed this into my own unspoken mantra: Don't think too far ahead. Don't rehearse every single step beforehand. Just do what needs to be done as the occasion demands. React to the conditions.

Mike kept the throttle wide open as he was told, and eventually we got out of there.

When we got back to the station I wasn't sure if Mike still liked me, if he respected my knowledge and experience, or if he thought I was nuts. Ultimately, that wasn't the point. We got through a situation that might turn out to be some of the worst he'd ever see, and he learned a lot.

CHAPTER FIVE

Short Tow, Long Tow

Two years after we arrived at Cape Disappointment, our second child Matthew was born. Courtney and I were slowly getting accustomed to life in this small town. We had a community, a group of friends to rely on, people our own age who also had children. On the weekends we had barbecues in our backyard. The house we lived in was located on a quiet street and came with a fenced-in yard that was perfect for kids. Although an ugly beige color, the house did stand almost on top of the water, facing the Baker Bay channel. We had the best view a job in the Coast Guard could buy. We could see small islands off the coast glowing phosphorescent in the sunlight. We had views of the river and the ocean, of boats passing by. On warm, sunny days we would stay out in the backyard all afternoon, barbecuing salmon, oysters, and clams, drinking beer, and watching the kids run around, playing games, laughing. These were the good times, the ones that are so clear in my memory even many years later.

While stationed at Cape Disappointment I ran every day and was in the best shape of my life. Running half marathons and marathons and 10k races balanced my life, the stress and adrenaline of work and the demands of fatherhood. Every morning, regardless of the weather, I got up before the sun and ran six miles. There were trails behind the station that went up into the hills of the Cape Disappointment State Park (formerly known as Fort Canby State Park) overlooking the Pacific, where old World War II bunkers were dug into the cliffs. There I moved like a shadow beneath the cypress and pine, in the dappled early-morning sunlight and in the soothing rain. You could see almost everything from up there: the Cape Disappointment Lighthouse, the A Jetty, Benson Beach, the Columbia Bar, the boats plying back and forth by Buoy 10. The ocean looked much calmer from that perspective, not so malevolent or frightening. From up there, you could almost let yourself imagine the ocean was peaceful.

My first big case was a long tow. It was late 1999, right after I was coxswain-qualified. I want to say it was in late November because we were getting heavy wind and rain from the south. We got the call around dinnertime. The SAR alarm went off and I heard my name called over the intercom, telling me to report to the communications room. I was excited.

When I reported to Comms they gave me the situation and the details they knew about. A big crab boat forty miles offshore had just broken down, but there was no major distress reported. The swell wasn't rough, maybe seven or eight feet, with twenty-knot winds and on-and-off rain. I got under way with my crew, knowing it was going to be a long night.

It took us just over four hours to get to the crab boat while high above us the clouds moved like surf. The boat was in a pretty calm spot in the water where there was no swell or waves to complicate things, although it was raining steadily and it was cold. We threw them the heaving line with the towline attached and they tied it down to the bow of their boat. I told my crew to put two turns on the tow bit and to start letting out more line. Within twenty minutes we were on our way back to the station.

We made our way back slowly, going maybe five knots. I had the crewman let out seven hundred feet of towline very gradually. It was all going exactly how I'd imagined, exactly as I'd planned. When we got within a mile of the coast, we had been out on the water nearly nine hours. I was tired, and my nerves were rubbed raw. My eyelids were twitching.

The sun slowly rose, eclipsed by the low hills to the east. The crew was taking shifts sleeping and keeping watch on the towline. I hadn't been paying attention, just trying to stay awake and keep my bearings. When we got to the entrance gates, we still had seven hundred feet of towline out, way too much. Suddenly I realized I didn't have full control of the boat. I slowed down to three knots and the crew started shortening the towline. Then, we heard it: a resounding boom, the sound of metal scraping on metal. The crab boat's helm turned and it started going hard to port. Their steering wheel was stuck, causing the boat to corkscrew around the towline, twisting it, sending everything off course. We tried to pull in more towline to straighten them out but it wouldn't budge.

Their boat was heading right for the wooden gates, the massive pilings at the entrance to Baker Bay channel. There was no other choice but to hammer the throttles down and turn the boat sharp to starboard and just pray, hoping the line would straighten out. One of the crewmen started calling out the distance from the gates to the boat.

"Fifty feet . . . forty feet . . . thirty feet . . . twenty feet . . . ten feet."

I closed my eyes and braced for impact. I didn't want to see what was going to happen next, even though I was sure I couldn't stop the sequence of events at this point. I would wreck the boats. The passengers would drown. My crew would drown, though of course I would be the one to come away, unharmed, and live with the guilt of having killed five men and ruining their families. I would be dishonorably discharged from the Coast Guard. I would be exiled to an island off the coast of Alaska, where I would spend the rest of my days, drunk and guilt-ridden.

"Holy shit!" was the next thing I heard.

I opened my eyes. The big boat had somehow slipped past the gates, missing impact by less than a foot. We were both in the channel now, but the only place to put the crab boat in side tow was in front of the station. The towline was still all twisted up, and the crab boat was drifting to port. It was still a job, but we got the boats moored and tied to the docks. The clouds had broken up and a light breeze was blowing down off the hillsides. I had been up for nearly fifteen hours now. I was freezing, shivering. I changed out of my dry suit and into my uniform. I was exhausted. I needed a shower, some food, a nap. I needed to go home to my family.

Out of the 430 cases I was involved in at Cape Disappointment, about half of them were boat tows and escorts. Most of those boat tows were routine, a simple matter of tying down some line, letting out enough towline, and guiding the craft back to the closest boat basin. Some tows, however, took up to twenty hours, like when we had to tow those big tuna boats that sometimes got disabled seventy miles offshore. There were no commercial tow services they could call to pull them in; we were it. And we got calls regardless of weather and sea conditions.

Only a few of the tow cases I worked were extraordinary. Only a few were cases where we pushed the envelope, where we towed seventy-foot fishing vessels out of surf zones with twenty-foot breakers and seventy-knot winds and rain so thick you could barely see past the bow.

The most significant tow of my career took place on January 29, 2001. And while it wasn't necessarily a boat tow, it was still the biggest surf I had ever seen at the Bar.

The afternoon before, Courtney and I had had some friends and their kids over for a barbecue. My friend Kaleb Adkins, a break-in surfman, had a daughter and a son, the same ages as Taylor and Matthew. It was a rare day, at least by winter's standards—sunny and warm and not much wind. The kids and the dogs played in the backyard. We ate and we drank. We looked out at the water, shimmering green and gold in the sunlight. We talked about the steelhead season, about sports and boats and surfing and waves. It was the first time any of us had seen the sun in a couple weeks, and we were trying to make the most of it. We knew it wouldn't last. There were reports of a big storm blowing in from the northwest, heading for the coast, where it was supposed to hit later in the week. Crab season had been open for almost two months now, at least since early December, and the commercial fishermen were just beginning to make their quotas.

The storm hit earlier than expected. Later that night, after everyone left, the weather took a quick turn. Heavy rain swept the coast, blown by gusty winds of up to fifty knots. Swells approaching twenty feet bathed the cliffs and beaches outside the Columbia Bar. This wasn't unusual weather for this time of year, and we all knew it could get worse.

At 0530, the Air Station in Astoria received a distress call from a fishing vessel disabled in the turbulent seas twenty miles offshore. It was taking on water. A couple minutes later, the Coast Guard station received a call. Soon after that I got a call at my house from the watchstander on duty. I was still half-asleep in bed when I picked up the phone. I didn't have to be on duty for another couple of hours.

"Why are you calling me?" I said.

There was a pause on the phone.

"We've got a boat broken down twenty miles offshore, taking on water," he said.

"How many people on board?"

"Four."

"Why doesn't the on-duty surfman go?"

"Well, we . . . ," he started to say. "It's over the boat limitations."

I looked at the clock. I wasn't quite ready for this. *Over the boat limitations* meant the conditions exceeded the 47's standard capabilities, which were sixty-knot winds and twenty-foot waves. It meant the boat and crew would take a beating. He knew I'd go.

"I don't have to report for duty for another two hours," I said.

"Well, I guess we just wanted to see if you wanted to go," he said. "Since you're the oncoming surfman."

"Okay," I said. "I'll go."

It wasn't that I wanted to go, but neither of the on-duty surfmen wanted to, and I knew if I didn't go, no one would. I also knew the conditions must be pretty bad if no one was willing to go out. I told the watchstander to call Kaleb and get me a good crew together, and I would meet him at the boat docks in fifteen minutes.

I hung up the phone and cradled my face in my hands. I must've fallen asleep for a few minutes because the next thing I knew, Courtney was nudging my shoulder.

"Do you have to go in?" she said.

"Yeah," I said.

"When do you think you'll be back?" she asked sleepily.

"Probably later tonight."

I got dressed and drove to the station and met with the watchstander. He asked if I wanted to go to the watchtower to check the conditions. I knew I wouldn't be able to see anything, so there was really no point.

"I want you in the tower," I said. "At least until we get under way and transit the Bar."

"Roger."

"Any new information?" I asked.

"No," he said. "The boat is still taking on water. The pumps are having trouble keeping up."

The sixty-five-foot fishing vessel, the *Pacific Sun*, based in Warrenton, was reported to be twenty nautical miles west of the station, though we didn't have a precise position. At the docks I met with Kaleb and the rest of my crew, an engineer and two others. There wasn't much to tell them; they knew we had to be prepared for anything. We got geared up and were soon under way.

It was still dark at 0600 when we left in the forty-seven-foot motor lifeboat. We couldn't see a thing except the small pool of light from the spotlight that fell on the water before the bow of the boat. The water was a brackish gray color covered here and there by thick clumps of seaweed and kelp. Despite the weather, all was quiet. The silence was unnatural. It seemed to magnify the sound of our voices, the clank of the boat rushing through the oncoming water, the static blurring on the radio, the wind and the heavy chop of the waves.

As we transited out of the Baker Bay channel toward the gates, there were eight-foot breakers at the entrance. "Have you ever seen anything like this?" Kaleb asked, reading my mind. I shook my head. The waves were never supposed to get this big here because it was protected on three sides by peninsulas and jetties and small islands. I told my crew to put on their helmets and their surf belts, to clip in. At this point we were all aware this wasn't going to be a routine case. They knew if we pulled this off, it was going to take a long time.

The weather buoy was reporting swells over thirty feet with 70 mph winds. Kaleb, who was prone to seasickness, was anxiously chewing on a Jolly Rancher. My experience made me good at predicting weather patterns; I could figure out swell periods, wave size, wave speed, when the tide was coming in, when it was going out. The tide was pushing in at this point, with waves at twenty-five to thirty feet separated by twenty-second intervals. I told my crew to stay alert.

Search and rescue isn't a simple matter of seamanship, of guessing the right combination of boat speed and physics to get through tough situations. I would eventually leave it because of the damage it did to my body and my nerves. It beats you up like playing in the NFL. No one can do this job forever; it's impossible to put your body through this much stress for very long. It wears you down, all of it—the dead bodies, the fear, the violence, the sheer physicality of it all. There's hardly a surfman I know who hasn't had some kind of metal plate or screw surgically fused to one of their broken bones. Eventually, everyone breaks. I did, but not until later, three years after this tow, when I was still living high on my fantasy.

Out of the rain and mist, the large shadow of a towering wave rose up above us, the size of a three-story building. I felt the boat ride up the face, catching air at the top, then quickly descend down the back side, as if riding a liquid roller coaster. As we exited the channel and entered the

Bar, the watchstander called in over the radio and asked if we were okay. He said he had lost visual on us behind a wave for about thirty seconds.

"We're fine," I said. "If anything happens, you'll be the first to know."

"Roger," he said.

From the gates of the Baker Bay channel to the entrance buoy of the Columbia is about eight miles. It took us two and a half hours to make the transit, which meant we were only making two or three knots per hour, which was slow compared to our normal response speed, which could be up to 28 knots per hour. It was well over the limitations of the boat. The tide was flooding, meaning it was incoming, rushing into the river. We were pummeled by wave after wave, each one bigger than the last. For two and a half hours we would hit a couple of waves, get pushed back fifty yards, crawl forward a hundred yards, hit a couple waves, and so on, two steps forward, one step back.

It felt like I was backing down on the throttles more than we were going forward, and there were moments when I thought the entire boat was falling apart. It shook and rattled and vibrated; it sounded like the bolts were coming loose. There were moments I thought we should turn around and call it, but even if we'd wanted to, there was no way I could turn around in this weather. The waves at the Bar were thirty feet and the wind was blowing fifty knots. The cold rain bit our faces.

The scale of this place is something to marvel at, to gaze upon and be amazed by its power. Time has carved the land and the ocean here into many inlets and bays. The geography allows the waters of the Pacific and the Columbia to roil and mix and churn, scraping and sifting earth into something both violent and elegant.

Once we got out of the Bar, it was 0830h, and we still had a little more than twelve miles to go until we reached the *Pacific Sun*. We were going slowly, but it was getting light enough to see where we were heading. In the gray early-morning light the waves looked much bigger than they had at night, their large, menacing faces bearing down on us. I knew we probably shouldn't have been out there, but I had developed a certain image of myself as a man of ability, a person with drive and purpose. We were the only boat within a hundred miles willing to transit the Bar and venture into open ocean in this weather. We were being hammered by giant walls and towers of water, the boat driving down the backs of waves, free-falling thirty feet at a time, plunging into the water, with whiplash jerking our bodies back and forth. My arms were getting tired and my face was stinging with the onslaught of tiny bullets of mist and rain. Out there, there was no feeling other than that of being alone, a speck on the ocean, miles from nowhere.

Around 1015h, we had visual with the *Pacific Sun*. I remember in the distance it looked like nothing more than a toy model. It was disabled and taking on water twenty miles northwest of the entrance buoy. I knew my decisions would determine what would happen with this tow, and the first was the most important, as it would form the basis for the others.

We got on scene at approximately 1030h. I circled the boat a few times from a safe distance to assess the situation, to make sure there weren't any punctures in the hull. We were no closer than fifty yards away, with no way to get any closer. There was a long period swell pushing in, and we continued to ride thirty-foot swells.

I got the captain of the *Pacific Sun* on the radio. His boat was taking on massive amounts of water now, he said, with some fear in his voice. The water was flooding faster than the pumps could handle because the bilge pump intake lines were getting clogged. There was also partial flooding in his engine room, which was making the boat unstable and difficult to handle in this weather. My best guess was that the water was coming in through the shaft seal.

There was no way we could pass him a pump in this weather, no way we could get close enough to take the boat in tow, not without crashing the boats and capsizing both of us. We sat there for a while, talking on the radio, trying to figure out what to do. The helicopter from Group Astoria got on scene not much longer after we did, hovering right above us, steadying itself against the wind and rain, flattening the water with its rotors.

"What's the swell height down there?" the pilot asked over the radio.

"Somewhere between thirty and thirty-five," I said. To be honest, I had no real idea.

"That's what I thought," the pilot said.

There was static on the radio.

"Hey, we're having a hard time getting a reading here," he said.

There was more static. Then, a set came and the *Pacific Sun* disappeared behind a wave, which carried us in the opposite direction.

"Where'd it go?"

"Do you have visual on the *Pacific Sun*?" I asked.

"Roger," the pilot said. "They look to be okay." Static. "What's the course of action here?"

"Give me a second," I said. "Stand by."

I radioed the captain of the *Pacific Sun*.

"What's your status?" I asked.

"The fish hold is flooding with water," he said. Now his voice was trembling. "The pumps are barely keeping up."

I tried to calm him as best I could.

"It's okay. Just sit tight and listen. Is the engine room flooded? Can you drive the boat still?"

"Yes, I can drive," he said. "But it's not easy."

"Okay," I said. "That's okay."

I radioed the pilot. "Okay, we're going to escort the *Pacific Sun* back to our station. No need for aerial support."

"Roger," the pilot said.

I radioed back to the captain and told him the plan. He seemed suspicious of it, but I told him there was really no other way, unless we all wanted to just stay out there until the storm blew through or got worse, which could take a couple hours or a couple days, you never knew.

"Okay," he said. "Roger."

We started making a slow transit back to the station, taking extra precautions. While I had escorted boats across the bar many times, I had never done so in such weather. As their escorts, we acted as their security blanket, a guide finding the passage to the nearest safe haven. The *Pacific Sun* followed behind us at a safe distance. My crew was exhausted. I was exhausted. We had been under way for nearly eight hours. It was 1100h and we had many miles and hours to go. The swell was still big but the wind had calmed some. I told my crew they could relax their helmets and surf belts for now. I listened to Kaleb chewing on a Jolly Rancher. His eyes were half closed. He rested against the helm of the boat, close to falling asleep in spite of the spray of rain and water pelting his face. A dense fog started to gather over the Bar.

Once we were a few miles from the entrance buoy, a call came in on the radio. It was from a crab boat waiting out the storm near the entrance buoy. They'd seen us passing and asked if they could follow us in. I rogered. Then another call came in. Then another. It seemed there were about nine or ten fishing boats that had gotten stuck outside the Bar and were trying to make it back in when the storm hit. These boats were waiting for the storm to pass because they couldn't make it in safely but once they saw us they decided to follow us in across the Bar. They all started lining up behind us, one by one, like ducks or quail crossing the road. By the fourth or fifth call, I just picked up the transceiver and told them all to fall in line.

"You ever seen anything like this?" Kaleb asked.

"No," I said. "Never."

Still true to this day.

When the weather was like this, a second lifeboat was always dispatched. Usually, it hung out on the Bar, just outside of the surf zone, in case something bad were to happen to the first boat. When we saw the other motor lifeboat, it was standing by at the entrance buoy, everyone suited up with all their gear. We must have looked ragged to them. We had been out on the water for nearly eight hours. Our faces were chapped and wind-burnt and our feet were kicked up on the dash of the helm.

The boat driver operating the other 47 called in over the radio. "Jesus," he said. "This is huge. I've never seen breakers this big here before."

"You should've seen it this morning," I said.

"What's going on? Where did you pick up all these boats?"

"They were just sitting outside the Bar at the entrance buoy," I said. "Waiting for us, I guess."

The swell had calmed some by now and there was no more wind, now that we were closer to the Baker Bay channel. I looked behind and saw a long line of nine or ten fishing boats following in our wake. The other 47 took up the rear. We drove through the gates into quieter steel-gray waters that mirrored the sea. I listened as it slapped the sides of the boat. It was still raining too.

The other lifeboat relieved us and escorted all of the fishing vessels back to the boat basin in Warrenton. There were no casualties and few injuries, no major damage done to the boats. When we got back to the station, I changed out of my dry suit and into my uniform, filled out and submitted my report. I don't remember what I did next; my memory goes blank here. I might have talked to Kaleb about the case or I might have gone home, where I might have had a beer and sat in the living room, watching TV. I can't remember. What I do remember, though, is that my hands wouldn't stop shaking for the next two days. Every surfman has a first big-wave case. This one was mine.

Later that night and through the next day I was jittery and anxious, pacing around the house, trying to soothe the feeling of exhausted nerves, the combination of terror and exhilaration. After the *Pacific Sun* case I had a clear understanding that at any moment I could be shattered by the ocean. The only thing to compare it to is a sense of dangling inside a void, of standing at the edge of a cliff and staring down. I recognized it as the feeling that I had finally arrived—I'd done the work of a true surfman.

The storm lasted for four more days.

There are short tows, and long tows, usually remembered by the size of the boat involved, the location, or the hazardous conditions. Then there are some that are memorable for the people involved.

One day when I was a new surfman we were just starting lunch when the search-and-rescue (SAR) alarm went off. I looked up at Kaleb who just shrugged and threw his fork down on his plate, as if that decided it. We left our lunches and walked over to the communications room. The watchstander called down, briefing us on a call he'd received about a woman falling out of a boat.

Kaleb and I got in the utility boat. We drove out of Ilwaco toward Astoria, where the woman was in the water. The boat she had fallen out of was nearby. I got on the radio and told the boat what the plan was. They were panicked, but I reassured them that everything was going to be fine. We were going to pull her out of the water and escort their boat back to Astoria. They were all in compliance.

But this wasn't going to be a textbook case.

Kaleb threw a life ring out to the woman and she grabbed on and we pulled her toward our boat. That was the easy part. Because she was a big woman, the two of us couldn't get her up over the side. After a while, we gave up. It simply wasn't going to happen. We told the woman to hang on tight while we came up with another plan.

"What do you want to do?" Kaleb said.

"Give me a second," I said. "Let me think."

I looked around the boat. There wasn't any need to rush because there was no immediate threat to her life. She had a life ring. The likelihood of her drowning now was almost none; there was plenty of time to think.

I looked from Kaleb to the woman and back to Kaleb, trying to come up with a plan of some kind. It needed to be easy and efficient, no complications, no mess.

"Get the lines," I said.

"The lines?" Kaleb asked.

"Just get them," I said.

The plan was to wrap a couple of lines around her and fasten her to the starboard side of the boat, as if we were doing a routine side tow. We cinched a rope around her stomach to stabilize her and gave her another one to hold on to just in case something else happened. I could tell by the look on her face that she was little embarrassed, but Kaleb and I did everything we could to reassure her. And so we towed her just as if she were a boat and not a person lashed to the side of ours, cruising slowly along the Bar, making a couple of knots an hour. I was trying to time the boat over the waves, so the woman didn't get slapped against the boat too hard. The other boat followed right behind us. I told them on the radio that I was going to bring her back to the station, to make sure she was all right.

We got the woman out of the water when we arrived at the docks and gave her a towel. Her boyfriend came up to me, a short guy with glasses and a Prince Valiant haircut.

"Thank you, sir," he said.

"It was really no problem," I said.

He was magnanimous, smiling. "Thank you so much," he said again. "You saved her life."

I didn't, I know I didn't. She would've been fine, even if I weren't there. She would have lived either way. But I also didn't correct him. I was young and enjoyed the admiration from those who had only passing knowledge of our work. I hadn't yet learned of all the things that could possibly go wrong, all the mistakes and guilt and regret that came along with being a search-and-rescuer. In the meantime I was enjoying this man's gratitude and praise. He reached out and we shook hands as he thanked me one more time. Then he turned around and walked away with his arm around his girlfriend.

I went home later that night with feelings of intense satisfaction and gratification, not thinking about the real questions that would only begin to surface some years later. Had I truly saved her? Was my work as a surfman in the Coast Guard truly making a difference in people's lives? Perhaps I'd gone on believing that for the next few years.

Perhaps I'd gone on thinking that all of this was true.

CHAPTER SIX

The Graveyard of the Pacific

THE COLUMBIA RIVER BAR HAS A LONG AND TRAGIC HISTORY. SINCE records of ship movements in the area began in 1792, the Bar has claimed over two hundred ships and many more lives. There was the fishing vessel (f/v) *Bettie M*, sunk by the A Jetty. There was the *Isabella*, a Hudson Bay Company supply ship, sunk off of Sand Island. There was the *Peter Iredale*, which ran aground at Clatsop Spit, the remnants of which are still there. There was the steamship *Admiral Benson*, with its crew of sixty-five and carrying thirty-nine passengers, which was stranded in the sands of Peacock Spit, near the mouth of the river, and pounded by heavy squalls. Peacock Spit itself is named for the wreck of the USS *Peacock*, an eighteen-gun, 115-foot US Navy sloop that grounded there in 1841 and was torn apart by currents and surf. Of the shipwrecks that came before 1792 not much can be said, though it is not a stretch of the imagination to say there were numerous others from the earliest days of maritime travel and trade.

I'm not sure where the nickname "the Graveyard of the Pacific" came from or who first coined the term, but it isn't wrong. The Columbia River Bar is not just a graveyard for boats and lost lives, but for stories. The stories that get told leave a legacy; they live on in us and become codified as myths, as parables and lessons, as signs of warning and hope.

Here is one that keeps returning to me. We got a call from a crab boat named *Gypsy* around 1500h in the summer of 2002. I recognized the boat and the crewmembers as local fishermen, people I knew of. I'd seen them at the grocery store, at the bars, just driving around town. There were three guys on board who reported that they'd had a huge fire in their engine room. They gave us their position, no more than a half-mile outside the Bar.

Crewman Ken Ritvo and I were already out on the water, patrolling the Buoy 10 Fishery in one of the utility boats, making sure all the fishing boats had their safety equipment and were fishing legally, so it only took us ten or so minutes to get on scene. Once we got out of the Bar and into the open ocean, we could see the fire. Thick plumes of smoke were rising from a half-mile offshore.

As we approached the fishing vessel, one of the guys on board came over the radio and said they had gotten most of the fire contained, but that one of the crewmen needed medical attention immediately. This was the guy who had opened the door to the engine room, and when he did there was a backdraft that made a fiery explosion, blowing him back several feet. There were no broken bones or sprains, but he had burns all across his face. The smell, I remember, was thick, acrid, a mixture of blood and smoke and burnt hair and skin. His hair was burned off completely, his eyebrows and everything. The skin had melted off his face, bubbling in places, and the whites of his eyes were full of blood. I wanted to look away, but I couldn't stop staring. I drove the boat alongside the f/v *Gypsy* and Ken helped the guy over the side. He sat down and Ken gave him a blanket and a life jacket and told him to hold on tight. I told Ken to sit behind him to make sure he was secure.

"We're going to haul some ass now," I said.

"Okay," he said. "No problem."

On our way, the guy was cool, nonchalant, talking to us as if nothing had happened, as if his face hadn't just been burned off. He was in shock, but conscious and awake. Every time we hit a wave or a small bump in the water, he let out a big whoop of delight.

"What a great day," he said.

I agreed. It was a nice day, sunny, mid-70s, little wind, and calm waters. The guy put his feet up on the side of the boat and laced his fingers behind his head, now bald. He didn't seem to be in any pain, except for a pretty bad cough.

"Great day to get your face burnt off is what I meant," he said.

He might've been smiling, but I couldn't tell because of the burns on his face.

"How do I look?" he said, with a cough.

"Well," Ken said. "I don't think you need to get a haircut."

The guy laughed, coughed, laughed.

"You guys busy today?" he said.

"Not really," Ken said. "This is our first real emergency."

"I guess I should say you're welcome then," he said.

When we got close to the entrance gates, I radioed Comms to discuss options. They asked if we needed any helicopter support and I told them no, it would take too long. We decided to just take him back to the station, where EMS would be waiting to pick him up.

"I'm sure you guys weren't expecting anything like this when you woke up this morning," the guy said.

"Not exactly," Ken said. "But I guess that's part of the job."

"That's right," he said. "Always ready."

He coughed some more.

Within fifteen minutes of picking him up, we dropped him off at the Camby boat launch area, where an ambulance was waiting for us. We helped the guy over the side of the boat and onto the pier. The ambulance crew lifted him onto a gurney and gave him an oxygen mask, sliding him into the back of the ambulance. Just before the ambulance took off down the road, he sat up and waved to us, giving us a thumbs-up.

I thought he was going to be okay. When we picked him up off the *Gypsy* he seemed fine—at least as fine as was possible after an accident like this. He still seemed to be doing well when the ambulance drove him off to the hospital. But I later heard that on the way to the small postage-stamp-size hospital in Ilwaco the man went into cardiac arrest and was without a pulse for fifteen minutes. It wasn't uncommon after this sort of accident. The smoke and fire had destroyed his lungs, irreparably. I heard they were able to revive him for a flight to a hospital in Portland, where he would go into cardiac arrest—and die—again.

When I heard the news, my heart sank and I felt sick to my stomach. So often in the field of search and rescue we never hear about what happens to the people we rescue. You have to move on to the next case, and then the next case after that. You do not have the luxury of closure. You must move on.

Ken Ritvo and I have stayed in touch over the years, calling one another every few months. He still lives on the Columbia River, but on the Oregon side, in Astoria. He is out of the Coast Guard now, working as a civilian, training boat pilots. Not long ago we were reminiscing about old cases and I asked if he remembered the guy whose face was burned off. Like me, he remembered the smell, the man's face, the bubbling skin, his odd sense of humor. Ken confirmed that the man had died in the ambulance and was resuscitated, but that he'd ended up making a full recovery at the hospital in Portland. When I remembered the details differently, he told me he wasn't actually 100 percent certain. Still, he was pretty positive the man was alive and well, despite his face, and living in Ilwaco. It made both of us feel better to believe this to be the case.

Most Coast Guard stories are grim because most of them are about life and death. They deal with fear, terror, and loss. They remind us of the insignificance of human beings in relation to the sea, and the vast, wild expanses of untamed forces that some venture into. At times they're about true heroism, the kind that takes place every day without an audience or expectation of recognition, the kind we acknowledge only among ourselves.

There was one story pretty much everyone in the Coast Guard knew, about MK1 Charles Sexton and the fishing vessel *Sea King*, which sank four miles northwest of the Columbia River Bar in 1991. This seventy-five-foot stern fishing trawler had four men aboard when heavy waves came up over the gunwales, steadily filling the engine room with water.

Sexton, a petty officer, along with a crew of four other volunteers, launched a motor lifeboat to help them, well after dark. A helicopter was launched out of Group Astoria, and after a failed helicopter hoist one of the men on board was injured. Sexton volunteered to go aboard the *Sea King* to treat the injuries of the crewmember, informing the flight surgeon of the injuries and providing first aid. He also assisted in the dewatering of the boat. While there are a few different ways to dewater a boat, Sexton knew how to operate the Coast Guard pump much better than the crew of the *Sea King*. With several pumps to remove the seawater filling up the engine room, he continued for six straight hours until the fishing vessel rolled without warning, throwing two of its crew into the ocean. The *Sea King* took another long roll to the port side and looked for a second like it was going to recover, but it didn't. The port quarter went under and the boat was capsized in seconds. Sexton, along with two of the fishermen, was trapped in the enclosed pilothouse, and sank with the vessel.

The Coast Guard erected monuments with his name; they named boats and buildings after him. The maintenance building at Station Cape Disappointment was named in his honor. I know it is wrong to remember him in this way, to valorize him and glorify his absence, to use his name as a battle cry to rally the troops. Rather than remembering him as a hero, I have too often thought of the person he never had the chance to become. I know it's wrong to think of him in this way, as well, but I can't help it. I can't help thinking of the fact that he would never have the chance to raise a child, watch them grow. He would never see his parents deepen into old age, never deepen into old age himself and watch his children grow into adults and have children themselves. He would never have the chance to look back on all those years with both pride and regret.

There was a saying in the Coast Guard after he died. It went, "Keep bright his memory so that the next time someone asks you who are your heroes, you won't hesitate to answer Petty Officer Sexton." What is the responsibility, I have often wondered, of keeping bright such a memory, of telling such a story? And whose responsibility is it? And a responsibility to whom—to him? To his family? To people like us?

Sometimes heroism is doing the jobs nobody else wants to do. That's the scenario that presented itself when a helicopter from Portland crashed near Camp Rilea in Warrenton, Oregon and Kaleb Adkins took the call. There was fog when it happened, thick as pea soup, which made everyone wonder why a helicopter was even out there in the first place. Apparently, it was one of two helicopters that a husband and wife had chartered to film part of a documentary about Lewis and Clark's exploration of the Columbia River. The wife's helicopter was the one that crashed. I was not on this case but I knew about it, just as everyone at the station did. It was pretty traumatic for everyone involved. Kaleb didn't talk about it, not for a while. I knew exactly how he felt; he simply couldn't get the images out of his head.

The way he described it, the call was almost like watching a movie in slow motion. When the search-and-rescue (SAR) alarm went off, he took a crew out in one of the motor lifeboats. They drove south along the coast through the fog. It was so still and quiet you could hear the water lapping rhythmically at the rocks on the coastline. It was hard to believe a helicopter had just crashed and burned; it just didn't seem possible. But soon, fuel sheen was visible on the surface of the water, then debris, wreckage. Large pieces of the rotor blades, metal and shrapnel floating here and there beside the boat and between the clumps of seaweed. Then came the body parts. The legs. The arms. A torso. A head. One of the crewmen leaned over the gunwale and started dry-heaving over the side.

The fog pushed in and a couple of helicopters were dispatched from Group Astoria. A rescue swimmer was lowered into the wreckage to pull out the body parts. The body of the woman was still beside the boat, and when the swimmer came to lift her onto the rescue basket, a swell came in and hit her body against the boat and her legs twisted and her torso popped off. There was just the top half of her body, and her head, which was cracked wide open. Blood was in the water, mixing with the fuel sheen. Years later, he would tell me he couldn't stop thinking about the color of her skin.

When the second helicopter with the husband got to the scene, Kaleb pivoted the boat to try to block their view of the body. There was a camera crew in the cockpit, and a young boy in the operator's seat, who Kaleb believed was the dead woman's son. When he told me about this case, he remembered locking eyes with the boy, staring right at him. He remembered that feeling of desperation, of wanting to shield the boy from having to see his mother like that, of wanting to save him from that image of her that would be seared in his mind forever, like scar tissue. But at that point, from the cockpit, they could see the rotor blades in the water, they could see the wreckage. The woman's flight jacket was bobbing in the water, among the swell of the debris. Kaleb saw it on the faces of the husband and the son: They knew. The flight crew knew.

Rarely do search-and-rescuers talk about the cases they've worked, and if they do, it is usually with someone else who was on the case with them, and mostly about what they could have done differently. Part of the job is about letting things go, about moving on, not getting caught up in one bad case. Back then, the Coast Guard had what they called Critical Incident Stress Management, or CISM. They were meetings for search-and-rescuers who had experienced any sort of trauma, usually related to death or some unbelievable act of violence. While only some of the sessions were mandatory, all of them were difficult to sit through because no one wanted to speak. Everyone sat in silence, waiting for others to speak up. The silence was always long and uncomfortable, and no one made eye contact. No one wanted anyone else to know how they were taking it, so everyone looked up at the ceiling or stared at the wall, hoping to do each other this small kindness. Sometimes I think the reason most of us joined the Coast Guard in the first place was so we could see and commit such acts so others wouldn't have to. So we could soak up all the violence and ugliness, all the cruelty, and wring ourselves out into the ocean.

Cape Disappointment is the closest thing to a home I have ever known outside of my hometown of Aptos. It was where I did a lot of my growing up. It was where I became a father, where Courtney and I rooted our marriage. It was where I discovered my vocation as a search-and-rescuer and where I met some of my closest friends, the kind of friends that I consider family. It was also where I met some of the most dedicated service members, people who understood the significance of what we were doing here.

I first met Jack Watkins in the spring of 1998, within the first few months of arriving at Cape Disappointment. Jack was a member of the Coast Guard Auxiliary, a small branch of unpaid volunteers in Ilwaco—mainly retired fishermen who own boats—who are dedicated to the search-and-rescue community. Among them, no one was more devoted than Jack Watkins.

A retired commercial fishermen, Jack had a boat called the *Baymist*. He was a husband, a father, and a grandfather. When I first arrived at the station, he helped train me as a watchstander and later as a Comms watch. By the time I arrived he had been volunteering for over ten years and had helped train countless people. He even stood watch himself once a week.

Jack and I became friends over the course of several years. We had similar interests, like golf and fishing. His *Baymist* was a small, white twenty-six-footer with fishing poles always mounted on the stern. From a distance, it kind of looked like a small charter boat. He was always out on the water early in the morning, with very few exceptions, either taking a shift on the Bar boat or just cruising around, trolling for salmon. And he never failed to stop by the station to offer his help or let us know he was going out just in case we needed him for something.

When I had duty in the watchtower, I would radio his boat and ask what his heading was.

"Zero-zero-five," he'd respond. "Over."

That meant he had caught five fish so far that morning.

When I asked him what his position was, he'd disguise his location in geographic vagueness that we all understood as an inside joke. Fishermen never advertised their location over the radio when they were catching fish.

Jack Watkins died sometime around 2001. I'm not sure how he died, but I remember it feeling sudden: One day he was there, the next he was gone, and it felt like a vacuum had sucked out all the air from the station. The flag was at half-mast when I got to work that day. Everyone was in disbelief, mourning our collective loss. I was speechless.

Jack's death was pretty tough on everyone. Not only was it a sad month at the station, but it was a sad month in the town of Ilwaco. The sky seemed abnormally overcast for weeks. One Saturday morning, the weekend after he'd passed away, I woke up early and went for a run, longer than usual. I ran up the cliffs of the state park. I ran past the bunkers and down the cliffs and around Waikiki Beach and back toward the jetties. Then, rather than going back home to shower, I ran into town. It was my day off, so I didn't have much to do. I went to the small grocery store; I don't know why. I guess I just wanted to talk to someone else who knew Jack, someone who knew him better than I did. The grocery store was run by a husband and wife who had lived in Ilwaco for decades, and knew Jack, so I headed that way. But at the store a sign was posted asking for donations for Jack's family. I couldn't bring myself to go in. I turned around and went home.

There were no monuments erected for Jack Watkins; no buildings bear his name. There was a small funeral service held at the local cemetery for close friends and family. I didn't go to that service, and I'm not sure if I'm in any position to use his name in my book, but I also think that a book about my time at Cape Disappointment wouldn't be complete if I didn't mention Jack. He wasn't a hero by conventional standards. He didn't jump out of helicopters to rescue people, nor did he swim into heavy currents to pull people to safety. He was just a kind man who was generous with his time. He was the most dedicated Auxiliary member I knew. That's the way I want to remember him, and I believe that's the way he'd want to be remembered. I want to remember him on the *Baymist*, cruising the waters of the Cape, the wind whipping his thinning hair, the spray of water soaking his face. To this day, I can still hear his scratchy voice coming in over the radio. I still see him standing at the helm of his boat, waving his cap at me as he turns the corner and vanishes behind the jetty. More than anything, I believe he was someone who truly cared.

By 2002, I had moved close to the top of the station's totem pole, something I have always been proud of, despite the fact that it came with more paperwork and more responsibility. I was the head of the deck department, which meant I managed and supervised a crew of over twenty Coast Guardsmen, as well as the annual boat maintenance budget. My responsibilities included maintaining all aspects of the station's personal protective equipment as well as keeping the unit's three motor lifeboats and one nonstandard boat in Bristol condition. While I embraced my responsibilities, perhaps I didn't fully appreciate them at first.

One week that summer I was filling in for the CO who was out of town on a family vacation. This put me in charge of the day-to-day operations of the station. I enjoyed the authority of such a role, giving others instructions and having them follow through. The week was pretty uneventful, so it wasn't as if I was being challenged. Toward the end of the week we had a slow day that was nice: not hot, maybe mid-60s, and not a lot of wind. The swell was two or three feet with an occasional four-foot swell coming in.

At lunch I went down the A Jetty to surf by myself. Unlike the first time I tried to surf the A Jetty, I had learned to surf this spot when conditions were conducive. Before I left, I told Kaleb to keep an eye on things, and if anything came up, to just drive out to the jetty and flash his lights. An hour later, I saw one of the motor lifeboats speeding around the tip of the jetty and I could hear the SAR alarm going off. Then I saw Kaleb's truck come driving up the road, kicking up dust. He started honking his horn and flashing his lights.

We were required to have two lifeboats and a full crew on standby at all times. That day one of the boats was already on a case, towing a tuna boat back to Astoria. The other one had just vanished around the jetty. I paddled in, scaled the rocks, and got in the truck. Kaleb gassed it and we fishtailed in the dirt. There was a report of a boat capsized down near Seaside, he said.

"Any injuries?" I asked.

He said no.

"People in the water?"

"Not sure," he said. "Just got the call."

At the station, I grabbed a boat crewman and hopped on the twenty-three-foot utility boat, the fastest boat we had. I didn't have time to change so I put on a personal flotation device (PFD) life jacket over my wet suit and drove the boat south across the Bar, doing thirty knots. I cut across the South Jetty to save some time, which was something we wouldn't normally do unless it was totally necessary.

We beat the other lifeboat to the scene and started doing our search patterns, zigzagging across the water, trying to cover as much surface area as we could. There was no capsized boat in sight, which meant it had probably sunk already. There was no report of how many were on board the boat, so I wasn't sure what we were looking for. Soon, the 47 joined us, and within ten minutes, someone spotted a body facedown in the water. They tried to resuscitate him but were unsuccessful, so the boat brought him back to shore. From there, he was taken to the hospital, where the coroner said the man had been dead for at least fifteen minutes before we got to him.

Fifteen minutes. That was all. That was the difference between this man's life and his death. Even if the record shows there was little I could have done, I know in all honesty I failed in my duties that day. It's impossible not to think this way in my line of work, even years later. If I hadn't been out there surfing that day, if I had kept a closer eye on things at the station, maybe I could have made up that fifteen minutes. Fifteen minutes is an eternity in this line of work. Perhaps it's true I couldn't have changed the outcome of that capsizing. Kaleb was a reliable surfman who was more than capable of running the station. On the other hand, perhaps it is true I cost someone his life because I wanted to go out to the A Jetty and surf that day. The point is that I didn't do everything I could have, and I made a mistake. By letting my guard down for just a moment, I had allowed these dark waters to claim another life. The one crucial lesson the Cape taught me again and again was, "Anything can happen."

Sometimes the way we react to one situation or another doesn't matter as much as how we carry it. That is how we know who we really are. We remember the cases in which our resolve is put to the test, and we fail. That is when we see ourselves clearly for the first time, and ask ourselves the real questions, like, could I have made a difference that day? Could I have made a difference on any other day? Could I have been better?

Just offshore in the Baker Bay channel there is a small piece of land called East Sand Island. It's a renowned bird sanctuary right at the mouth of the Columbia Bar where students from the local community colleges and from colleges in Portland often come to monitor the birds, their habitat, their population growth. One year we picked up the body of a dead woman who had washed up onshore there. Every year there were more missing persons reports than we got dead bodies, which made you wonder—where did all the bodies go that didn't come back? Most likely they got washed out to sea on an outgoing tide, or sank to the bottom, or got snagged on a rock and became food for the fish. The bodies we did recover, though I know it's hard to imagine, were the lucky ones.

This happened to a friend of mine, Ken Ritvo, a fireman and qualified boat crewman who served in the navy before coming to Cape Disappointment. He did two six-month-long deployments traveling around the globe, both times on an aircraft carrier, and was trained in arresting and launching recovery equipment. He decided to join the Coast Guard only a year after leaving the navy and had to endure the two months of boot camp in Cape May, New Jersey. When he arrived at Cape Disappointment he had only the slightest knowledge of this place's reputation. This was one of the first cases he worked and one of the first dead bodies he'd picked up.

The station received a phone call one winter morning from a college professor saying someone in his class had found a dead body washed up on East Sand Island. Comms relayed the call to the CO, Matt Swain, who with Ritvo took the call and steered one of the twenty-five-foot safe boats out in the channel. There was no dock to tie up the boat on the island, so they drove the boat up onto the sand close to shore and waded onto the island from there.

When they found the body, she was lying faceup in the sand on the beach. Her blonde hair was tangled in seaweed. She was fair-skinned, in her early thirties, maybe younger than that, wearing nothing but a bra and acid-washed jeans. There were three- to four-inch cuts just below her wrist line. The body was still pretty fresh, likely dead fewer than twenty-four hours. Matt Swain walked over, stood over the body, and looked down.

"Yeah, pretty sure this one's dead," he said.

All of us in the Coast Guard have to find ways to deal with death and Matt Swain was no different. Swain radioed the Clatsop County Sheriff's department which sent a deputy out with a coroner to process the scene, including taping off the beach, taking photographs, and collecting evidence. The coroner confirmed the time of death was within twenty-four hours and the cause of death was blood loss.

The sheriff's department later told Ken that the woman was from Spokane. She'd bought a one-way plane ticket to Portland, rented a car, and drove out to the coast. The sheriff told him they found a receipt for a kitchen knife purchased from the Safeway in Astoria in the center console of the rental car. The car was found parked at the base of the bridge. The kitchen knife was never recovered, but they assumed it's what she used to cut her wrists. They also assumed she had jumped off the bridge.

This kind of stuff wasn't rare during that time of year, in this part of the country. The rain and bad weather grates on the nerves. One year, the station in Newport got a call from someone who said they thought they saw a woman throw a child off the bridge and drive away. Whoever reported the call wasn't wrong. The child was a four-year-old boy, the woman's son, whose body was picked up that same morning by the Bar boat. The mother was picked up by police officers not long after that and convicted.

After the scene at East Sand Island was processed, Swain and Ritvo put the woman in a body bag and waded back out into the shallow water. They carried her to the sheriff's boat. When they lifted her up and tried to heave her over, Ritvo banged her head against the side of the boat. "Sorry," he said, though it wasn't quite clear if he was talking to Swain, the sheriff, or the woman. "Sorry," he said again before they lifted her over the gunwale and placed her on the deck.

At a busy station where there's a very active fishing and boating community, those of us in the Coast Guard pick up plenty of dead bodies, on average two to three a year, though there were occasions when we would pick up four or five within days. I've even picked up the bodies of a few children before, and even though it was always difficult, I never had a real issue with it. I'm sure most who have served in the military would say something similar. It is not that I think we learn to deal with death or cope with it differently, but that we simply stop seeing it after a while. We push it to the edge of our vision. I grew to think of it as a consolation to their families to return their loved ones. I can't say for certain if that was true, or if it was just my way of dealing with an unpleasant task.

Traffic on Christmas Eve is not surprising, but one year when Courtney and I were driving home across the Astoria-Megler Bridge after picking up some groceries at the supermarket across the river in Astoria, there was a car blocking the road up ahead, and several cars lined up behind it. We were one of the last cars in line. I figured it was just last-minute holiday traffic, people doing the same thing we were doing.

As the traffic slowly thinned I could see a guy standing in the middle of the road, trying to direct traffic. He looked like a normal guy because he wasn't wearing any reflective or construction gear or anything like that, just jeans and a sweatshirt.

"What do you think happened?" Courtney said.

"I don't know," I said.

That wasn't entirely true.

"Maybe a car accident?" Courtney said.

"Yeah," I said. "Maybe."

I knew what had probably happened, what had most likely happened, but I didn't want to say it out loud—not in front of Courtney or the kids. Up ahead, two people stood at the edge of the bridge, looking down as traffic inched forward. The guy in the middle of the road directed us to go around the car that was holding up traffic. It was parked off to the side, one of its wheels on the curb. As we drove past, I looked over and saw a little boy, no more than three or four years old, sitting in the backseat with his seat belt still on. He looked confused. He was looking around the car and outside, through the open window. I swear he looked exactly like my son Matthew, though that might have been my imagination. There was no one sitting in the passenger seat or the front seat, either.

It took us almost a year to recover the body of the man who jumped off the bridge that day, leaving the boy in the car, and we only found him by accident. The currents in this part of the Columbia River were always unpredictable due to swell and tide and wind, which made it impossible to tell which direction a body might drift.

It was low tide when we found him, tangled up in one of the pilings of the bridge, wrapped around the rocks and cement. The tide was sucking out, fast. I was on the Bar boat, patrolling alongside the bridge. It had only been a few months since 9/11 and our unit still had orders to search for bombs or anything of a suspicious nature on the Astoria-Megler Bridge. It was our job each morning to check every one of the 171 pilings that support the bridge.

Right where the bridge dips down toward the water a charter boat found the body of the man and called it in. Considering he'd been in the water for almost ten months, it was strange that he hadn't traveled very far. He was in pretty bad shape. His skin and flesh were in the later stages of decay, almost like he'd been sent through a meat grinder. Countless lacerations and bruises covered his face and arms and legs, where his skin had been exposed to the weather. His long, wiry hair was plastered to the wooden piling.

When the boat crew picked him up it looked like he could burst at any moment. I was worried we were going to tear his skin open because he had absorbed so much water, which isn't an irrational thought. Once we had pulled a decayed body that was lodged in the rocks of some cliffs. Yanking too hard on the rope ripped his stomach open, and I watched as his guts spilled out into the water.

Taking precautions, the boat crew lifted the man's body onto the boat secured him to the deck, and brought him back to the station. The CO called the authorities in Astoria and arranged for the body to be taken to the coroner.

I like to think that the families of those whose lives have been taken by the Columbia River are thankful they have a body to bury. The families of those never recovered have to live with the knowledge that their loved one is still out there, cast adrift on the sea. They have to live not knowing where their loved one is, buried somewhere in the watery graveyard of the Columbia River Bar along with so many others that had come before them, their final resting place unmarked and unknown. I like to think that when we picked up a dead body, we were providing some of these families with a small sense of closure. There is no way to really know.

A couple weeks after we found the man tangled in the bridge piling, I went for a run through the state park. It was a busy winter that year. I remember a lot of the cases, a lot of the bodies, at least two suicides we pulled out of the water within the span of two or three weeks. I ran to relieve some of the stress, to get out of the house, to avoid thinking about it. We didn't talk much at the station about the cases we worked, and I didn't talk much about it at home. Part of it, I'm sure, was that none of us wanted to show any weakness. So we removed ourselves from it. We internalized it. We said, "I'm good," or "I'm fine," and that was it, as if that resolved the matter for us.

When I got to the top of the hill that night, I was out of breath. The fog had rolled in, snaking through the hills and the trees and hovering over the town. It was a few days till Christmas and I could see the vague glow of the lights in town uplifted by the fog. It was quiet. The crickets chirped in the dark. Far below, the waves crashed against the cliff and the Christmas lights looked like a smear across the town. It was a faint color, glowing red, turning from orange to yellow and back to red. The colors seemed almost glossy against the night. From up there on that hill, it looked like the entire town was on fire.

From left to right: Riley (our dog), Courtney, Matthew, Chris, Mia, and Taylor D'Amelio. Tuckee Tahoe, 2008

Surf training, circa 2005

Surf training, Siuslaw River, 2005

AFRAS Awards with Congressman Sam Farr, 2002

AFRAS speech

Surf training, Yaquina Bay, Newport, Oregon, circa 2000

Surf training, Siuslaw River, 2006

This is where Mia decided to take a nap (and almost gave me a heart attack).

Surf training, Siuslaw River Bar, 2007

Awards ceremony with Vice Admiral Thomas Collins and Transportation Secretary Norman Mineta, circa 2002

Surf training, Station Siuslaw River, 2006

Association for Rescue at Sea (AFRAS) awards presentation

Siuslaw River Bar crossing

Surf training, Umpqua River, 2008

Surf training, Umpqua River, 2008

Coast Guard Station
New Orleans, 2013

CHAPTER SEVEN

Worst-Case Scenario: The *Linnea*

On February 9, 2001, I had just finished running on the treadmill at work before going home for the weekend. The small gym at Cape Disappointment was equipped with weight machines and treadmills, stationary bikes and free weights. Everyone at the station was expected to put in time there, to maintain certain physical requirements. I never liked running on treadmills, but if I only had a brief amount of downtime while on duty I usually ran there rather than the cliffs at the state park. I was on the second day of a two-day shift and was about to go home for a couple days off. It was evening, just after it got dark, though the light was still rosy with dusk. Outside, the air was cold and wet and it was raining lightly, or misting. I was tired from two long days of duty but felt that high after my run. Halfway between the gym and the mess deck the search-and rescue (SAR) alarm went off. My name was called over the intercom, asking me to report immediately to Comms.

Although my shift was nearly over, the alarm pumped adrenaline through my body. I hopped in my truck and met a crew in the change-out room. BM3 Gene Marshall was the break-in coxswain, MK3 Steve Hayes was the engineer, and Ken Ritvo was my crewman, one of the most reliable we had. When it came to being a crewman, he knew his towlines, bridles, shackles, his firefighting equipment, pumps, his navigational tools. He was in the lounge watching TV, and right after the SAR alarm went off he met me at the change-out room.

"What's going on?" he said.

"Not sure yet," I said. "You'll know as soon as I know."

We stripped off our uniforms, geared up in orange dry suits, and were under way within three minutes. It was low tide, which made the boating dock pretty steep and the rain had made the platform slippery and hard to keep my balance. I realized too late I was still wearing my running shoes, but there was no time to change. We boarded the forty-seven-foot motor lifeboat and I gunned the engines to get us out of the channel as quickly as possible.

When I got the radio call from Comms, they said a sixty-foot fishing vessel was disabled in Clatsop Spit, taking breaks. They gave me the position of the boat, near Buoy 10. There were two passengers on board, but no injuries. It was clear the captain of the fishing vessel didn't know the Bar too well: Buoy 8 had been smashed in a storm a couple days before and was no longer there. The boat had been inbound, coming in from offshore, when the captain cut the corner from Buoy 6 to Buoy 10, rather than going around Buoy 8. They had been hit by a wave in Clatsop Spit and were now disabled in the surf zone.

As soon as we got to the gates we saw the boat a mile away, straight south. The pilot boat *Chinook* had been dispatched earlier to drop off a boat pilot on an incoming deep-draft boat, and they had stopped when they saw the fishing vessel caught in the surf zone. They were about a hundred yards from the disabled boat, the *Linnea*, and had bright halogens pointed at it that lit up the entire surf zone like a stadium.

The swell was breaking and sloughing. Wave sets were anywhere from fourteen to eighteen feet high, coming in three to four breakers at a time, with two- to three-minute lulls. I got on the radio and called the Bar pilot on the *Chinook*. We had to yell over the engine and the constant crash of waves just to understand each other. The *Chinook* couldn't get close enough to board the fishing vessel. There were too many crab pots in the water. The *Chinook* was the exact same boat as our 47, but twice as big and with a jet drive, which meant that if he ran over one of the crab pots, the engine would suck it up into the intake and they'd lose all power.

I eased the boat to the edge of the surf zone and turned to my crew and told them the plan: Get in there and bang boats and get the two people off. The *Linnea* was close to capsizing, with water running up over the gunwales, and the engine was fried. Its windows were all blown out. They weren't going anywhere.

"You guys think we can do this?" I asked.

Ken Ritvo nodded his head. The other members of the crew nodded their heads. They didn't look scared so much as nervous, maybe a little panicked. For many of them, this was their first case in heavy surf, and the fact that it was nighttime and pitch black didn't help.

The *Linnea* was about three football fields away, positioned right in the Buoy 10 Fishery, deep in the surf zone. Their area was lit up by the pilot boat, but for us, it was dark. The water was black. Even the air looked solid black. The rain didn't help our visibility either. We heard the waves well before we saw them. Once we got closer, I saw a wave feather close to our boat, the white water spraying off its crest, and as soon as I put my foot down to brace for impact, I felt myself shaking uncontrollably. During my time doing search and rescue I was scared only a handful of times—cases in which I felt the odds were stacked so high against us that our chances of pulling it off were so slim it was like a game of Russian roulette. In the field of search and rescue we call such cases "worst-case scenarios." It was not a good attitude for approaching this rescue, but it was realistic.

We hit six big breaks, then made our way to the *Linnea*. I was fatigued by the time we got on scene. My arms and legs hurt; my entire body ached. To make things worse, I realized the plan I had formulated wasn't going to work. We couldn't get close enough to the *Linnea* to get the passengers off; it was impossible. It just wasn't going to happen. The *Linnea* was a crabbing boat with hundreds of crab pots washed across the deck and over the sides. If we got too close the likelihood of sucking up a line was pretty high, too high to take the chance. We'd be disabled as soon as we got within twenty yards, and one thing I had learned as a boat driver was that you didn't want to become a part of the case yourself. It would be like a murder detective becoming a murder victim in the case he was investigating. So I stopped the boat and turned to my crew, trying to come up with another plan.

The *Chinook* still had their halogens on, which had been helpful earlier in locating the boat, but now that we were so close, the lights were blinding. The halogens lit up everything in front of and behind me. I pivoted the boat so the bow was taking the breaks, but when I looked forward to check for incoming waves, I was blinded. I couldn't see a thing. I got back on the radio and called the Bar pilot and asked him to turn off his lights. He said he couldn't do that. We argued for a while. I asked him again and he said no again.

By that time, I had way too much going on—managing my crew, calling out waves, and watching the lines—so I gave up. The new plan was to put the *Linnea* in tow. To this day, there have only been two boat tows that I know of that were performed with a 47 at night in breaking surf. The second one happened a few years later, on the Umpqua River. This was the first.

We worked as quickly as we could, which was pretty slow. Our boat was taking heavy breaks, making movement around the boat difficult. As the crew were wearing surf belts to avoid being thrown around, they were continually unclipping and clipping in, then unclipping and clipping in again. We were going to try a slip tow—an uncommon practice in the Coast Guard, only because it's impractical and oftentimes dangerous. It wasn't something we normally practiced or trained for. I had done it a couple of times before, but only on small recreational crafts—never on a sixty-foot fishing vessel, never in heavy surf, and never in the dark. I told BM3 Gene Marshall to go to the stern of the boat and throw the heaving line out to the *Linnea*, with the towline attached to it.

"You better not miss," I said.

He missed.

He tried again and missed again. We held our breath, watching, hoping each attempt would work. Everyone was anxious to get the rescue tow started. The longer we were out there, the more dangerous the situation became. Each attempt took time as we got slammed by oncoming waves and risked losing our position, losing whatever time the *Linnea* had left before it capsized and got swept away.

On his third attempt, he made it. The captain of the *Linnea* tied the towline to their bow and Ken Ritvo put three turns on the tow bit while the rest of the crew came up to the open bridge. I had Ritvo let out more line on the tow bit while we started to tow them out of the surf zone, still keeping tension on the line to create distance between the boats so they wouldn't collide. The crew was giving me updates on what was happening with the towline—if it was paying out, if it was pulling, where it was tending. He said we were towing the boat at a 45-degree angle.

"Brace!" I yelled.

A set came. A wave rolled in, feathering at its peak, and broke right in front of us. I squared the boat and got us over the wave and turned around to check the boat behind us. I turned the wheel to starboard to square the *Linnea* to the wave or we would've been dragged backward. It was like towing a giant sixty-foot anchor.

I thought things couldn't get much worse for us, but of course they did.

Ritvo noticed it first: a slight vibration on the boat. There were crab pot lines caught in the propeller. I radioed Comms and discussed options with the other boats, and we decided to head straight for Ilwaco, to the closest pier.

As Ritvo was paying out the towline, the tow reel started spinning out of control. Two hundred feet of line surged out, unspooling in about five seconds, and neither of the crewmen could get it under control. As it was spun the towline was smoking from friction against the aft deck. It looked like it was melting, turning to glass. In our haste we hadn't put enough turns on the tow bit and the tow reel had jammed. It gathered underneath the reel, clumping and piling up, wedged underneath. It was a rat's nest, the same way a fishing reel gets tangled up with line, but with far more dangerous implications.

There was no more line going out and we only had about three hundred feet between us and the *Linnea*, which wasn't enough. The strain was now all on the tow bit, and we could hear it beginning to pull at its mount on the stern. It made a grinding sound, metal on metal, like the sound of gears grinding. It sounded like it was going to tear the boat apart.

We hit a wave. Because there wasn't enough towline out, the *Linnea* was dragging us backward, back into the surf zone. I gunned the engines to get them over, but we were being held in place. I yelled over the crash of the waves. I told Ritvo to try and get the tow reel working again, to put a few more turns on it, but when he got down to the stern, he said there was nothing he could do. The line was hopelessly tangled. The tow reel was seized up with giant knots. I told him to keep trying.

In the meantime, I radioed Comms and informed them of our situation. It was perilous. They called in everyone who was available for emergency duty and both forty-seven-foot motor lifeboats and the fifty-two-foot Triumph were dispatched to help escort us back to the harbor in Ilwaco.

Crewmembers Ritvo and Marshall went down to the stern to untangle the towline and to set a tow watch. They were able to untangle enough of the line to put a couple more turns on the bit and then paid the towline out to four hundred feet. The other lifeboats met us at the edge of the surf zone, shining their lights, guiding the way for us. Due east of the Baker Bay channel were the "Jaws of Ilwaco." We called the entrance of the channel the "Jaws of Ilwaco" because there were old wooden pylons all over the shoreline that looked like teeth sticking up out of the water. We were going to put the fishing vessel into side tow once we got through the channel and into Ilwaco marina. But we were coming in too fast, going seven or eight knots. I hadn't been paying attention. My nerves were still shocked, and I was disoriented. We picked up speed: nine, ten knots.

Someone came in over the radio. It was the XO, Kyle Hoag.

"Two-four-eight," he said. "Check your speed."

Unlike small recreational crafts, big fishing vessels like the *Linnea* don't stop on a dime. They need time and distance to come to a full halt, and at the speed we were going they were headed right for the shore. They were going to pass by us and slam right into the pier. Baker Bay channel is narrow, and there wasn't room to moor up the boat, much less slow it down, back up, and put it in side tow. I couldn't see or think straight, yet I made a split-second decision: I put the boat in reverse and told Ritvo to go back down to the stern and start pulling on the towline, retrieving any extra line still out there. This allowed the *Linnea* to come right up to our port side where we threw them two lines, which they attached to their starboard gunwale so they were secured to us. Then I slammed both engines, trying to pivot the boat. I radioed the *Linnea* to tell them to brace themselves. I put the port engine all the way in reverse and gunned the starboard engine and turned the wheel to port side, hard as I could. Our boat jerked left and came perpendicular to the *Linnea* just as the *Linnea* swung around our boat to the starboard side. When they finally came to a stop, they were moored up. It looked like I'd planned it that way, like we did this sort of thing every day.

There was nothing routine about this case. It was a perfect example of Murphy's Law: Everything that could have gone wrong did go wrong. The *Linnea* had all its windows blown out, the engine room was flooded, and the intake was clogged. There were no severe injuries, though my crew was pretty banged up with bruises and welts, their faces wind-chapped and fatigued. However, I also knew that in spite of how bad things went, it could have been even worse.

Several months later, my crew and I would be recognized by an awards committee for our performance, our bravery, and courage in the face of extenuating circumstances as we confronted possible death. Although I had made a mistake that could have cost several people their lives, things just happened to work out for the best. Awards committees always seemed to ignore the fact that we could have just as easily been chewed to pieces and spit out. By some amount of sheer dumb luck, we managed to get out of it, relatively unscathed.

Once we were done and the boats were tied up to the pier in Ilwaco, I inspected the lifeboat and noticed that the only real damage was to the tow bit. It had deep ruts in it, as if a wild animal had clawed at it, trying to tear it apart. By the time I got back to the station, completed debriefing, and filled out my report, it was around 2200h. Drizzling rain was still falling steadily.

I changed and drove home, the car quiet but my head reverberating with the aftershocks of the rescue. The house was empty, cold, and bright as I turned on lights and walked around. Courtney was out of town with the kids, visiting her parents in California. I called her. I wanted to hear her voice. It must have been pretty close to midnight. She sounded tired, like she had just woken up. I felt hollow, loopy but was wide awake. Words were slow to come out of my mouth. She must have heard something unsteady, nerves trembling in my voice.

"What's the matter?" she said. "Are you okay?"

"Yeah," I said. "I'm fine. Just got back from a case, is all."

"Did something happen?"

"No. Well, yes. I don't know," I said. I couldn't explain.

There was a long pause, pregnant with silence. We listened to each other breathing on the phone for several moments.

"Chris?" she said.

"I'm fine. I just wanted to tell you and the kids I'm okay."

"Okay. I love you," she said.

"I love you too," I said.

I could feel my arms shaking when I hung up the phone. My legs were shaking, too. I put on some music and cracked open a bottle of whiskey. I sat down on the couch and took several big gulps, staring at the TV, which was turned off.

I didn't sleep all night. I was antsy, anxious. It was difficult to comprehend what had just happened, to calm the nerves that were so recently stretched to their limits. I paced around the house, from empty room to empty room. I stayed up until it got light out and watched the sun rise over the hills. I didn't have duty that day, nor did I have to go in the following day.

Finally, at around ten that morning, I fell asleep. I'd been up for the past thirty-two hours.

I slept like a dead man.

CHAPTER EIGHT

Helmets on Dead Men

His skin was white, almost translucent, a light purple shade where some of his blood vessels had burst. One of his eyes was half-closed, the other, wide open; his lips were upturned, as if he was smiling. His eyebrows were dark and thick, his nose curved, most likely broken. His jawline had a light five o'clock shadow. His black hair was slicked back as if he had just combed it, and there was a slight tear on one of his ears, where a fish had probably taken a couple bites, then given up. There was a small red gash across his chin, quivering in the water.

He was lying facedown in the water when we found him. He'd been there for a while, an hour or so, maybe more, before we even got the call.

I drove the boat right up alongside him, being careful not to bump into him or get him caught in the propellers. One of the boat crewmen went down and looped a rope around him and pulled him up onto the deck.

This happened in late 1999, just after I'd qualified as coxswain. I was still fairly new to the station, still working toward my surf qualification. Because I was still young, only twenty-five or twenty-six, I never thought of the bodies we picked up as people. I still thought of them as just that—dead bodies—not something anyone would care to maintain in good condition.

I was still learning.

We drove back to the station with the body. The sky was a steel-gray color, the color of most winter days in the Pacific Northwest. There were large squalls hitting the rocks farther north along the coast, and farther west along the horizon stood a fog bank, looming. But where we were was pretty calm. The waves were small but choppy, with a light wind blowing whitecaps off the surface of the water. I imagine I wouldn't have remembered any of this if it weren't for the sound of his body thudding around the deck, his head smacking the side of the boat every time we hit a wave.

When we took the man's body off the boat his head was cut up pretty bad, in worse condition than when we'd found him. His head had started to swell in places around his eyes and cheekbones. His neck looked like someone had tried to cut it off with a knife and had done a poor job of it. As soon as the CO found out, I got called into his office and was chewed out pretty good, but it was still nothing more than a hard slap on the wrist.

"Think about it," he said. "We can't bring a body to the coroner that's gotten the shit kicked out of it by one of our own. It looks bad for us. As well as the fact it's frustrating for them. You hear me?"

"Yeah," I said. "Roger."

I understood. He was telling me basically to take better care of the bodies, which was something I hadn't really thought about before. At the time I merely thought it was my job to rescue victims in distress, to save lives, not to care for those who had already lost theirs. Although it wasn't quite an official regulation, after this it became unwritten policy at the station that whenever someone picked up a dead body, they were required to put a helmet on them, to keep their face and head in pristine condition. I began training all of the break-in crewmen in this manner, emphasizing the importance of caring for the dead.

The next time I picked up a body was only a month or so later. We got a call about a body in Peacock Spit, someone who'd slipped off the North Jetty and was swept out by a wave. It was summertime, I remember, because summer is transfer season in the Coast Guard, and there were a lot of new faces at the station. I took three new crewmen out in a motor lifeboat. When we got the man's body in the boat, I sat him up on the deck. I lifted up his head, cradling it, and gestured to the crew for help.

"Someone come and help me put a helmet on him," I said.

It was a new crew and they looked at me, confused.

"What do you mean?" one of them said.

"Put a helmet on him, so we don't mess up his head," I said.

"But isn't he dead?" someone else said.

"Yeah, but it's our job to take care of him," I said.

They were still looking at me like I was crazy. No one made a move, so I gestured to one of the crewmen and he came over and handed me a helmet. I put it on the dead man and laced the strap beneath his chin, tightening it. For a moment, it looked like the man was still alive, until his head fell forward and then backward, as the boat was hit with a small swell. I gave the helmet a couple knocks on the head to make sure it was secure.

"Okay," I said. "Now we're ready."

CHAPTER NINE

"Always Ready"

EVERYONE REMEMBERS WHERE THEY WERE THE MORNING OF 9/11.

I was on duty, lying down on a couch in the officer of the day (OOD) berthing area, four doors down from the mess deck. I was trying to sleep before I had to go out on morning Bar boat duty. It was still early, before sunrise, and a soft gray light was falling through the window on the far side of the room. On the Pacific Coast, the news reached most of us well before the morning had fully awakened.

There were footsteps coming down the hallway, then a knock on the door. It was BM2 Sarah Merriman, a good friend of mine, and the only female boat driver at the station. Sarah was also the second woman in the history of the Coast Guard to be qualified as a surfman. She told me to come quick and turned back down the hallway. I got up and followed her down the hallway. She said the tower was on fire, smoking.

What tower—the watchtower? I asked. I was still groggy, tired, my head stoked with the heavy fumes of dreams.

She just shook her head as we kept walking.

Outside, the air was cold and wet and a thick morning fog was hovering just over the ground, running its fingers through the grass. Everything was in dark blue shadows.

I stood in a room with eight or nine other coworkers and watched the footage replay over and over again: The plane struck the tower, then there was an explosion and black smoke poured into the sky. I looked around the room. Everyone's eyes were glassy, unblinking. Whispering, each of us cautiously asked one another if we knew anyone in New York or had any relatives there. I felt my hands trembling at my sides, something like impulses being sent out from my core. I wanted to do something; we all wanted to do something. We were lifesavers. We felt helpless having to stand there and watch.

"You have family there, sir?" someone asked me.

Yes, I said. My entire family on my dad's side lived there.

Then the second plane hit and everyone went dead silent. More smoke, more fire on the TV. When the towers fell no one spoke a word. I didn't know what to think. I don't think any of us did. It was especially hard to grasp that it was a terrorist attack, a threat to national security. We were numb, nothing but witnesses. There was nothing we could do for those people.

Sarah held her hands over her mouth as if she were choking or holding back a scream.

After a few minutes, the silence was broken. "Holy shit," someone said.

The Coast Guard motto is *Semper Paratus*, "Always Ready." The months leading up to 9/11 were a busy time of year for the station, but the months following were abnormally busy. The Coast Guard implemented several major changes in the aftermath of the attacks that made many uncomfortable at Cape Disappointment. Once part of the Treasury Department, the Coast Guard now became a branch of the Department of Homeland Security. Orders came down from Washington, DC, and through the district commander and Group Astoria, telling us to shift our focus away from search and rescue and toward law enforcement and preventing potential threats to national security. A wave of fear and paranoia swept over us as it did the rest of the country.

We took on more work. Our commander put in a bid to put a gate around the perimeter of the entire station, and concrete barricades were erected. An armed guard was posted at the entrance to the gate, as well as one outside the commanding officer's house. I was pretty high up on the chain of command at this point, so I never pulled duty to stand guard. Remembering my time working cleanup details on board the *Sherman*, I felt sorry for the poor souls who pulled guard duty. Most of them were kids, nineteen, twenty years old, new recruits, standing alone at the gates beneath a halogen lamp, all night long, armed with 9mm Beretta handguns.

I disagreed with many of the changes that were being implemented at our station, as I thought our resources and manpower were being misused, but there was nothing I could do about it. I said nothing and toed the line. I even volunteered to stand guard at the gate a few nights a month. One night I was there listening to the waves beat against the cliffs, staring into the dark, at nothing, thinking how crazy this whole thing seemed. Who was going to come out all the way to the middle of nowhere? What would any terrorist want with Ilwaco and a few old fishing boats? *Look out for anything suspicious* was our only directive; we weren't given any other specific instructions of what we should be watching for.

A few months after the towers fell we received orders to increase our law enforcement and to start doing routine security patrols every morning and every night. Someone believed that the Astoria-Megler Bridge could be a potential target for a terrorist attack because of the Columbia River's importance in maritime trade. This meant that another boat crewman and I took one of the utility boats out along the bridge every morning, looking for anything that might be a bomb: charges, timers, wires running up and down the pillars. I was clearly out of my depth, as I had no idea what a bomb might look like. We never found anything, but were ordered nonetheless to continue our security checks along the bridge for the foreseeable future.

An engineer from Group Astoria instructed our station to focus our inspections on the pilings under the bridge. He believed this was the most likely place for a bomb to be planted. I had a hard time explaining to him that we weren't fully trained for law enforcement, for finding bombs or bomb removal. The middle of the bridge stood on a sandbar, and there were over a thousand pilings spanning the length of the bridge. Some of the pilings we couldn't get to because of the depth of the water, and if we checked each and every piling it would have taken us a half of the day if not longer. After 9/11 things at the station were never the same, but by the end of the year we stopped checking the bridge for bombs and, at least for a while, returned to some sense of normalcy.

The first time I met one of the most notorious fishermen on the coast was during the opening of crab season in 1999. He was based out of Hammond, Oregon, across the Columbia, and owned five boats that earned him millions from every part of the Oregon and Washington coasts, and even off Alaska, west and north, far into the Bering Sea. We heard he broke fishing regulations time after time and was well known among the fishing community as a kind of maverick, someone who would double-cross his brother for the right payout. Everyone knew his reputation as the world's greatest fisherman, but also for having a drug habit, and picking a lot of illegal crab pots. I didn't know how much of that was true, but knew he wasn't well liked. We'll call him the Captain. He ran a sixty-foot crab boat called the *Beast Coast*.

During this post-9/11 law enforcement phase we were patrolling the waters east of the station, moving south along the A-M Bridge, then coming back northwest along the Oregon coast, past Astoria, Warrenton, and Hammond. It rained on this particular morning and the storm still gathered on the mountains around us, and the green on the hillsides darkened and shined as the clouds moved and changed directions.

The emphasis on law enforcement had consequences for the town and the people in it because we were required by quota to board more boats and write more citations for fishing without proper licenses, for expired registrations, for failure to carry proper safety equipment and the like. There's a reason I was always so resistant to doing law enforcement, and that's because I believed, as some others did, that we were wasting our time and our resources. I felt like a maritime mall cop.

Due to this new direction in our work the attitude of the people in town changed dramatically toward us, and I couldn't blame them. Our station wasn't meant for law enforcement. We were highly trained specialists in search and rescue, boat crewmen and boat drivers who spent years dedicated to safety, not boarding boats and writing tickets. Despite feeling that this directive disrespected our station, our crew, and our training, I followed it.

We all felt tense on this day as we approached the *Beast Coast*, not really knowing what to expect from the Captain with his colorful reputation. Everyone at both Coast Guard stations on either side of the Columbia knew the boat, which was sixty feet long and had a menacing black hull. We were boarding the *Beast Coast* that day after getting a call for a disabled boat, then hearing an argument over the radio, including yelling, death threats, and the sounds of scuffling across the deck as two male fishermen traded blows. They were a mile down the coast, just off Seaside. I was with two other crewmen.

The owner, the Captain, was shorter than I imagined, more weathered. He was wearing a yellow jacket over a pair of gray waders. He was slightly balding and his face was grizzled with a gray beard and the lines of a man whose life had been defined by years of hard labor at sea, relieved only by the occasional day of drunkenness at bars from Portland to Nome. I knew others like him from my years on board the *Sherman*, and most of his kind hated the Coast Guard. He was from an older generation that had fished these same waters years ago when they were less regulated and there was less of a Coast Guard presence. I'd heard, but wasn't sure, that he had spent time in prison for crabbing without a license, yet we knew for certain that he paid hundreds of thousands of dollars in fines for fishing violations, and those were just the times he had been caught. When we boarded his disabled boat it was obvious that he saw us as a threat.

"Is everything okay?" I asked. "Does anyone need medical attention?"

"Medical attention?" he said. "You Coast Guard guys are always so damn melodramatic." He stared me down. "You know, if you guys just got out of our way and let us fish, maybe some of us would actually be able to make a living," he said.

His stare dared me to provoke him further. Instead I looked around the boat. His crab pots were full of crab and there were still a few waiting to be pulled out of the water. Whatever the argument I'd heard over the radio, it had ended and the crew was back to work. Two men were on the deck shoveling the crab into the freezer hold while another was pulling out the last crab pots. The Captain coughed into his fist, looked at me and back to his crew, then back to me.

"You know what you guys can do if you really want to help?" he asked. "You can pitch in and unload these crab pots."

He had a good catch on board and wanted to unload it in Warrenton. I told him we'd help by towing him back to Warrenton, and he agreed. When we moored his boat in the boat basin, he ordered his crew to start unloading the crabs. I still wanted to know what the argument had been about, but figured it was best to leave it alone. The Captain was standing up on the bow, arms crossed, looking down at his crew and smoking a cigarette, barking orders. He looked like a small tyrant.

Two weeks later, I got another call over the radio while on patrol. It was the *Beast Coast* again, and this time the Captain and his crew were disabled near Clatsop Spit. He had requested a lifeboat to tow him to the dock in Warrenton.

Crab fishermen are a strange bunch in my experience, prone to acts of violence, especially when their livelihoods are threatened by people like the *Beast Coast* captain. Everyone suspected he fished illegally, depriving others of legal catches. In the mid-1990s, when a group of San Francisco crab fishermen and a group of local wholesalers came to an impasse on the price per pound, he led a rogue group of fishermen who set their gear and started fishing rather than honoring the situation his fellow fishermen were in. He fished alone for nearly two weeks while the others negotiated, and by the end his pots were stuffed with crab, for which he made a killing. Any fraternal bond that had existed between him and the Bay Area fishermen was broken. Given what I knew of these fishermen it amazed me that he hadn't suffered retribution for it.

The Captain already had trouble with the law, so the increased maritime law enforcement after 9/11 didn't help. He'd been cited for fishing outside of designated areas and for bringing in thousands of dollars' worth of cod the federal fisheries agency charged had been caught illegally off the Oregon coast. It wasn't that I felt sorry for him or believed in what he was doing. It's that I saw a sadness in him that I don't think he was aware of. He didn't have a lot of friends; he had burned a lot of people by this point, and was really the last of an older generation of fishermen. He believed he was being put out of business by the government, and he would do anything to keep that from happening.

This captain was something of a local legend among the fishing community, despite his bad reputation. There was no question he worked hard to become captain of a fleet of fishing boats. At age seventeen he bought his first boat, a salmon trawler, and with the money he made from salmon he purchased his first crab boat and his first crab pots. Within a couple years he had more crab pots, and soon added a shrimp boat to keep him working during the summer and fall. He had the sixty-six-foot custom steel boat *Beast Coast* built for himself and made millions pulling crab from the autumn and winter misery of Alaska's cold sea. I never talked to anyone at the station or in the fishing community around Ilwaco who thought well of him. Despite his hard-earned status, most thought he was shady, entitled, and untrustworthy.

On the afternoon that we towed his boat back to Warrenton he questioned me the whole way, haranguing me with criticism about the way I did my job. The current was ripping ten knots and the wind was whipping the whitecaps off the waves. There wasn't enough room in the boat basin to put his boat in a side tow, so I did it just outside the main channel. He clearly didn't like my decision.

"Why you putting me in a side tow out here?" he radioed.

"There's not enough room in the basin and the current is too strong in there," I said.

"This isn't the way I'd do it," he said. "I've been fishing for thirty years and I've never done it this way."

I wanted to punch my fist through the radio.

"Well, for the safety of everyone on board, this is the way we're doing it," I said.

"Okay. Whatever you say, boss," was his response. His voice was condescending, patronizing. "You know," he said, "I used to like fishing. Now I pretty much despise it."

Clearly he hated me by fundamental constitution. The uniform I wore stood for everything he was against: government interference, rules and regulations, permits, and licenses—pretty much everything that he believed was putting him out of business.

"Mother Nature isn't always cooperative," was something we always said, especially at Cape Disappointment. The weather wasn't the only thing constantly changing. The latest directives at the station weren't permanent, though they would last more than a year, making us suffer through ticket quotas and boat boardings and the endless paperwork of law enforcement.

Eventually new orders came down telling us to do security checks for commercial cargo freighters coming into the Columbia Bar, those traveling to ports further upriver in Portland and Kennewick and Klickitat. Now our main duties were to board cargo vessels, inspect crews, and check manifests, a nearly impossible task for a station maintained by barely fifty crewmembers due to the volume of work involved.

Every day anywhere from ten to fifty of the cargo freighters came through the Bar, each loaded with hundreds of shipping containers. Similar to inspecting for bombs on the bridge pilings, we were not clear on what we were looking for, so we performed our duties with the reluctance of children doing chores. We took no pleasure in this work, which made us no more than security guards in boats. We boarded freighters and gathered the crew in the cafeteria for inspection and ID checks. We checked manifests and took a quick look around the shipping containers. Most of the crews were compliant and understanding. We never ran into any trouble.

One afternoon the station got a call in the morning to drive one of the forty-seven-foot motor lifeboats and drop off a boarding crew on a four-hundred-foot car carrier coming in off the Bar and heading for Portland. No one at the station had driven up next to a freighter of this size before, for obvious reasons. A giant freighter with a draft this deep could crush a smaller boat like a toothpick. CO Matt Swain said it wouldn't be a problem, and told me he wanted to come along. He wasn't a boat driver, wasn't used to driving boats in waters like this, and didn't understand their capabilities or their limitations. The deep drafts of these freighters create a tremendous wake, and the resulting suction pulls surrounding water toward and under the ship. Even if the freighter was going seven or eight knots, I told him, I didn't think it was possible to get close enough. We'd be chopped into driftwood.

"Well, we'll figure that out when we get there," he said.

"Whatever you say," I answered. "You're the boss."

Once we got within fifty yards of the car carrier, it was like looking up at a giant wall of steel. I eased the boat closer to the port side of the ship, keeping the steering wheel steady using subtle movements. Our boat got sucked into the ship's wake. Over the radio, I called the Bar pilot who was navigating the freighter and asked him to slow down. He did, reducing speed to five knots. When we got close enough, they dropped a ladder and the boarding team climbed up one at a time. Once they were on board, I steered the lifeboat away from the cargo ship, but the undertow created by its draft held us in place. We couldn't budge, and the powerful force was slowly dragging us back toward the carrier. I had no control over the steering. I felt the helm wobbling and shaking, trembling. I called the Bar pilot again and asked him to slow down some more. He slowed to three knots. I punched the engine and felt our boat lunge forward, as if released from restraints.

When we got to calm, flat water, Swain turned to me and said, "That was a close one."

"You have no idea," I said.

The drive back to the station was uneventful. There were a couple of fishing boats hanging out just offshore, trying to catch the last of the salmon or steelhead swimming upriver to spawn, though it was a little late to catch anything. They had their flags at half-mast, and a cold autumn wind filled them. The fishermen waved at us as we passed.

Later that week, Don Chatterman, the head of the Department of Fish and Wildlife, called the station, asking us to seize the *Beast Coast*. He said it had been reported fishing illegally just north of the Cape Disappointment lighthouse.

Seizing a boat, especially a commercial fishing boat, was kind of a big deal. It rarely happened. It required a lot of busywork I wasn't interested in doing. Seizures rarely happened because nobody wanted to go through the hassle of the related bureaucracy.

The Captain wasn't on the *Beast Coast* when we seized his boat and towed it back to the station. One of his close friends, a man who looked equally as threatening and hateful of what I represented, was in charge instead. But Fish and Wildlife was correct: The boat didn't have proper documentation, as its commercial permits had expired. The fine was $75,000.

The Captain drove through the gates of the station to pick up his boat later that day, driving a monstrosity of a truck that looked like a giant red toy. He was livid, shouting and screaming obscenities at me. I was sure he didn't even recognize me. To him, I was just another faceless uniform. But he was absolutely right about one thing: Back in the day, this wouldn't have happened. Back then, his boat wouldn't have been seized. Back then, he could have gone on fishing with an expired license until he stuffed his pots full of crabs and his pockets full of cash. But times had changed. The dirty days of crab fishing were long over, and he was part of a dying breed.

Three years later, I heard the *Beast Coast* caught fire north of San Francisco, just offshore of the Marin Headlands. It took on water and finally went down for good off Newport, on the Oregon coast. Of course there were rumors that it was all for the insurance money, and that after he received the settlement he paid off his fines and bought a new trawler.

The Captain is still out there fishing to this day, still getting in trouble with the law. Just last year I heard he was facing more charges for unlawful fishing. He'd been caught offloading 54,000 pounds of illegally caught crab with expired permits and licenses. More than two decades have passed since my first encounter with him, and nothing has changed. He's still fishing the same waters, still trying to skirt law enforcement and fishing regulations. I was kind of glad to hear he was still up to no good. Despite his reputation I still think you have to admire a guy like the Captain, a man who has dedicated his life to a single pursuit: professional fishing. It is a difficult profession to make a living at, and an even more difficult one to last in. A guy like him has done everything in his power to adapt to the changing climate, both legal and illegal, to survive, knowing that one day soon his kind will be extinct. I respect him for that.

For Christmas 2001, I took leave for two weeks and Courtney and the kids and I went to California to visit friends and family for the holidays. I needed a break from work, and Courtney and the kids needed to get out of the house. Courtney thought it was good for me to get away from the station at least a couple times a year, and she was right. Even when I was off duty, it seemed like I was missing something, like work was beckoning, and there was always a case to pick up. Yet it was hard to escape given the amount of stress I was under, with the changes being made at the station.

The vacation was unremarkable. We saw friends and family, ate lavish dinners, and exchanged gifts. Although the hysteria of 9/11 was just beginning to wane, it still cast a shadow over dinner conversations. We shuttled the kids from one house to the next, with diaper bags and car seats and snacks and bottles and toys and wrapped gifts, from Courtney's parents' to my parents' and back again. There was hardly a moment to breathe.

If I were guilty of one thing as a young father working as a surfman, it was that I was never fully present at home, not in the early years. I may have been there physically, but my mind was always away at work, on the ocean, the waves, the boats.

Back in Ilwaco, a fishing boat capsized in Peacock Spit a couple weeks after our holiday vacation. To me it felt like Christmas came a couple weeks late.

Kyle Hoag received the call from a man who had spotted the boat from the beach. He drove his truck out to Waikiki Beach and parked it facing the rocks that form the A Jetty. There was a thirty-two-foot fishing vessel turned over in the surf. The SAR alarm went off and both of the 47s were immediately dispatched from the station, along with a helicopter from Group Astoria. The boatswain's whistle piped again and all available off duty search-and-rescuers were recalled to the station.

I got on the twenty-three-foot utility boat and drove out of the North Jetty to Benson Beach. BM2 Sarah Merriman, who was off duty that day but volunteering with an Ilwaco beach rescue crew, approached the fishing boat from the beach. There was no visual on any bodies in the water. Five boats were dispatched at this point. My boat and two others did parallel search patterns, sweeping the cove from one end to the other, finding nothing.

Kyle Hoag came in over the radio. "Do you hear anyone trapped in the hull?"

It was nearly impossible to hear anything over the thrum of the engine and the crashing waves and the heavy pounding of the helicopter's rotor blades.

"Negative," Sarah said.

Kyle Hoag got back on the radio and told the helicopter pilot to back off. As soon as the helicopter lifted up, we could just barely hear a faint knocking sound on the hull.

The waves washed the boat up on the beach, grounded in the shallows. Because the primary economy of the Pacific Northwest consists of fishing and logging, anyone worth his salt owns at least one chain saw. Sarah and another volunteer procured two chain saws from the fire truck and carried them out to the boat. They cut holes in the hull and pulled out two survivors, one of them unconscious. They got the people back to shore just before the tide rose and the boat was taken back out to sea, completely swallowed by the waves.

When a boat capsizes and becomes a wreck near the Columbia Bar, it is nearly impossible to comb through the wreckage to search for missing persons. It is dangerous. The waves push in and push out and sandbars are constantly shifting, so there is no stable ground to stand on. Standard protocol suggests we do not pursue any body recovery from a shipwreck. We can only hope for the best. Even though we rescued two lives that night, two others were lost in the boat, trapped in the cabin when it sank, and their bodies were not recovered. One of them was, eventually, but not for a couple years. (That was the body I helped to pull out of the rocks, the one whose stomach tore open, its insides spilling out into the water as we worked to recover it.) Sometimes we could only be this lucky. Most of the time, we never find the missing bodies.

That night, I went home to a quiet house. Courtney and the kids were asleep. The house was dark and the clouds swiftly moved past the kitchen window, heading east toward the mountains. I sat in the dark for a little while, drinking a nightcap. I felt the cool rush of the adrenaline gradually leaving my body. My arms and legs no longer shook, but my chest was still pounding. I listened to the rain in the leaves and on the roof and on the river behind the house, flowing west to where it touches the ocean.

CHAPTER TEN

The Peacock Spit Case

ON THE MORNING OF SEPTEMBER 2, 2001, I WOKE UP AS USUAL AND RAN five or six miles along the trails in the state park behind the station. Then I went out to the A Jetty to check the waves, then home, where I showered before heading off to the station for duty. Up on the watchtower, I looked out across the Bar, where a Bar boat was cruising, reporting wave height and swell period.

Mornings were usually pretty mellow, but that day we were getting a strong northeasterly wind pushing in the fog. It was Labor Day weekend, a mild, overcast day, and we had a huge northwest swell running in that had probably started somewhere up in Alaska a few days ago. The main channel was probably fourteen feet, sometimes bigger. Clatsop was fourteen to sixteen feet, with an occasional eighteen-footer. Offshore, there was a long, rolling Pacific swell slamming the Bar with a twenty-five-second period. Those were the kind of waves that hit the sandbar and jacked right up. Surf was breaking everywhere, except in the main channel. Peacock Spit was the biggest I'd seen it in a while. It felt like an omen of some kind.

By the summer of 2001 I had advanced to operations officer, which meant I had some seniority, but it also meant a ton of paperwork and responsibility, more than I liked or was comfortable with. Along with my normal duties, I took care of the Auxiliary and helped manage the boat budget and everyone's schedule. I was third in command at the station and was required to make decisions both big and small on a daily basis. Sometimes the power and authority seemed cool, but other times it frightened me. I worked in an office in what we called the Puzzle Palace, where Comms was located, on the second floor. It was called that because of all the questionable decisions made there over the years.

When I got to the station that morning, I checked in at Comms and told them we were going to need a Bar boat out on the water all day. No one wanted to go out. Everyone knew it was going to be a long day and wanted to pace themselves. I volunteered and gathered a crew together. We checked the surf conditions. The weather was out of the ordinary for the season because the air was still, no wind or rain, just that huge swell that made the boat feel like a crib rocking over an abyss. From the A Jetty to the South Jetty there were a few stray fishing boats cruising around the Buoy 10 Fishery, but most of them came back in pretty quickly after realizing how big the swell was.

We'd been out there for an hour or so when we received a call for a capsized boat off of Benson Beach. We were circling around the A Jetty, so it only took a few minutes to get on scene where there was debris not far from shore still being pushed in. I called it in and said I was going in to investigate. We made an inbound run, negotiating the waves. We must have been pretty close to the beach because the boat started kicking up sand and the Fathometer stopped working. We started seeing the wreckage, and then, two bodies, facedown, too close to shore for us to get to. The near-shore current was moving five or six knots, so the bodies flew right by us. We couldn't get to them.

I called in the two bodies and exited the surf zone while waiting for a helicopter to arrive. Once we got back to the station another boat went out to patrol. We refueled the boat and I went to shower and change clothes. I was soaked and couldn't stop shivering. At lunch I was talking with Kaleb Adkins and BM2 John Warren in the dining area. The TV show *Cops* was playing in the lounge, behind them. Then the station commander came down to talk to me about the case.

This CO was fairly new to the station and not well liked, which wasn't entirely his fault. Most of us at the station treated newcomers like this, with caution and an uneasy disdain, especially if it was the brass. The way we saw it, he was just a pencil pusher and didn't know the first thing about how a heavy-weather surf station operated. He never made qualifications as a surfman and seemed to always have a chip on his shoulder about it. He walked around the station with an air of insecurity and overcompensation. He was short and stocky and had gray hair and a mustache. We didn't really get along.

"You guys got pretty close to the beach out there," he said.

"Yeah," I said. "We couldn't get in much closer than that."

"You looked pretty close to grounding the boat," he said.

"Yeah, but I didn't," I said.

The CO sat down next to Kaleb, directly across from me, and changed the subject. He asked about the bodies and the body recovery. I told him the helicopter crew from Astoria had taken over the scene when I left.

"Kind of a bummer you couldn't get to those bodies," he said.

"The helicopter picked them up," I said.

"Yeah, but it would've been nice to pick them up yourself," he said.

"I wouldn't say that," I said. "As long as someone picks them up. You always want the family to have some closure."

He was goading me, patronizing me, trying to get me into an argument. Nobody wants to pick up a dead body, and I was happy to leave the task to the helo crew. Yet I always felt it was one of the most important duties of my job: to recover bodies, dead or alive, at least for the sake of the family, to have closure. When a body is lost at sea, families are left to live the rest of their lives antagonized by the mystery of never knowing, wondering where their loved one is from one moment to the next, drifting somewhere in the Pacific, alone. That not knowing always seemed unfathomable to me.

I finished eating my lunch and packed a pinch of chew into my lower lip, wintergreen Copenhagen.

"Goddammit, Chris," the CO said. "How many times do I have to tell you not to chew inside?"

"I don't know," I said. "Are you sure you've told me that before? I don't remember."

"I've told you at least ten times," he said, getting red-faced.

"Really, I don't think I've ever heard you say that before."

He smiled at me.

"I'm telling you now," he said.

"Okay. Maybe I'll remember this time."

He got up and patted me on the shoulder.

"Good work anyways," he said.

After he left I stayed in the cafeteria for thirty minutes or so, talking sports with Kaleb and Warren. It was baseball season, time for the October playoffs. We were making predictions and placing bets.

After lunch, I was heading to Comms when I heard the pipe. The watchstander told me to report immediately over the intercom. It sounded more important than usual, so I ran up the brick stairway. The CO was in the communications room with the phone to his ear. He looked at me with real concern, the kind I only saw on the rarest of occasions. Whatever it was, it was bad.

"What's going on?" I asked.

"The radio just cut out," he said.

"What? What do you mean—what radio?"

He walked past me and sounded the search-and-rescue (SAR) alarm and piped a boat crew to the docks. He'd just gotten off the phone with Group Astoria, who had just received a call from a pleasure craft that had gotten caught and was broken down in the surf zone in Peacock Spit. They'd heard someone on the boat say, "Oh shit!" right before the radio cut out.

"What's their position?" I asked.

"No specific position. Somewhere between the Cape D Lighthouse and the North Head Lighthouse."

"Okay. Stay on the line here," I said. "See if you can get a better position on the boat. And get Warren on the radio and tell him to get back to the station as soon as possible."

I bolted down to the boat docks. Warren had gone out on the Bar boat after lunch. It was just past noon and we must have had nine or ten cases already. The rest of the station was occupied; all of the other boats were running cases around the Bar, towing fishing boats out of the swell to basins further inland. As I ran down the gangplank I saw the Bar boat pulling into the docks, tying up. Warren met me at one of the 47s. FN2 Jerry Giles and MK3 Robert Wallace were the fireman and mechanic on board. I was still in my working blues and asked Warren to drive us out of the channel while I changed into a dry suit.

The Peacock Spit case became blown out of proportion in the months that followed. There was a lot of talk that it was one of the biggest cases of the year, at least one of the most high-profile. There was a lot of media attention surrounding it, and the case became a story of huge success, of great heroism and bravery. The crew would be commended for their acts of courage, nominated for awards and medals. But to me, none of this was real.

In retrospect, I believe our case got a lot of attention for a few reasons. The primary reason is because there was a helicopter and a rescue swimmer dispatched to the scene. But I also believe that, after the events of 9/11, when the towers fell, it left a void at the center of our communities. We were searching for any reprieve, grasping for anything that might provide comfort or hope. This rescue fit perfectly into our shared need for those heroic stories.

Once we got out of the Bar I told my crew to clip into their surf belts and to keep their eyes open. The visibility was good but it was getting cold, the wind was increasing to a howl, and the waves were wild, spraying mist ten feet high, the whole ocean roaring, clawing, and frothing like a hungry caged animal. We hailed the other boat over the radio but it was all static. No sign of the imperiled boat or wreckage could be seen.

We got to the tip of the North Jetty when there was a lull in the swell, so I cut the corner, and we were met with a set of seven towering waves. The bow of the 47 pointed up to the sky, then pivoted and dropped like a rock, again and again. We started a broad, general sweep moving north by northwest looking for any evidence of the wreck, but found nothing. We drove farther north and west and still found nothing. We doubled back and started doing another search pattern, this one running parallel to the coastline, where we were met by another set of massive waves.

Once we got over the last wave, Warren yelled out over the bow that he had a visual on the boat. It was capsized, completely turned over, with its hull coming out of the water, getting beaten by waves about four hundred yards off our stern. I turned the boat to starboard, figuring we'd gotten pretty lucky here. We could have driven right past it.

As we closed in on the capsized boat, one of the helicopter pilots came in over the radio. I saw the helicopter hovering fifty feet over the water coming in from the south. They were on scene before us. They saw us approaching from the east.

"Looks like we got the forty-seven coming in," the pilot said. "Let me know if you can get in this far. They're right underneath us."

"Roger," I said. "Just give me a minute to back up."

I turned the boat around and tried backing down to them, but it was taking too long. We hit a set of breakers and the waves washed over the sides of the boat and across the deck. The crew braced themselves against the railing.

"Two-four-eight, we've got a visual on four people hanging on to the hull of the boat," the pilot said.

The radio cut out for a moment and there was only static.

"Can you see them?" the pilot said.

"No," I said. "That's a negative."

We were in a blind spot. We drove over a wave before the capsized boat came into our sight again, this time in full view. I assessed the extent of the damage. The boat was completely turned over, with its hull facing up, and there were four fishermen clinging to it, taking on breaking surf. I could hear the wooden planks beginning to split and crack.

"I have a visual," I said. "Over."

I turned the boat around again and made a beeline toward them. While we were making our inbound run, the pilot came over the radio and told us we should back off—a set was coming in.

"You might just want to stand by," he said. "These are pretty big breakers."

"I think we'll manage," I said. "It's pushing fifteen feet. But I think we'll be all right."

We got within thirty yards of them and hit three more waves, and then there was another small lull in the swell. I eased back on the throttles and inched my way closer to the capsized boat.

"I can't tell from up here," the pilot said, "but it looks like they all have their life jackets on."

"I'm not sure," I said, "I don't think so."

It was difficult to keep the boat stable, pointed into the oncoming waves, and try to evaluate the situation, never mind come up with a rescue plan during the brief glimpses I had of the men in the water.

Another set rolled in, lifting the capsized boat and dropping them out of sight, then lifting them up again and dropping them down in the trough. I had to back off to avoid bumping the boats, but it looked like one of them didn't have his life jacket completely fastened to him. It looked like he was just lying on top of it. He wasn't moving much, but he looked alive. All four of them were still alive.

"This is fucking intense," the pilot said.

"What?" I said.

"This is fucking crazy," the pilot came again.

"Roger."

The communications room from Group Astoria radioed in, requesting a status report.

"Two-four-eight is on scene," the pilot said. "We've got a boat turned over in the surf zone. Four people overboard. All appear to be alive. Standing by with the two-four-eight. We are both trying to get these people off the boat. Over."

I got as close to the capsized boat as I could without slamming into it. I told Warren to go down to the stern and get them to swim toward us so we could toss them a life ring. He unclipped his surf belt and made his way to the stern, yelling over the waves and the heavy thwack of the rotor blades, waving his arms at them, trying to coax them off the hull of their boat. Their boat was on the verge of breaking apart, especially with the swell picking up, the wind howling, and the lulls between sets becoming shorter. They were getting hammered.

The capsized boat was struck by a wave and I heard the hull crack, splitting at the bow. One of the men started floating away, the swell pulling him away from the boat. He was the one without a life jacket on.

"We just lost one off the boat," the pilot said. "Repeat that: We just lost one off the boat."

Over the crashing din of everything—the waves, the wind, the shouts of my crewmen, the shouts over the radio, the rhythmic beat of the helicopter blades, the engine of the boat thrumming—I heard the other three men who were still clinging to the boat yelling and screaming his name.

"Looks like he just let go," the pilot said.

"We can't get to them," I radioed. "They don't want to make the swim."

"Roger that," the pilot said. "What's the plan then?"

We decided to have a rescue swimmer get to them. The rescue swimmer, Alan Damico, was lowered from the helicopter on a hook and cable and dropped right into the surf zone. We watched as he was pushed twenty-five yards in the other direction, then swam over to the man without the life jacket, who was floating facedown in the water not far from the boat. I could see him struggling to keep his face out of the water and taking in large gulps, so I started to pivot the boat toward him to see if we could get close enough to throw him a life ring. The swimmer got to him first.

Damico, the rescue swimmer, covered more than ten yards to the port side of the boat, swimming with the nearly unconscious man underneath his arm. Crewmen Warren and Wallace went down to the leeside to help lift the man up onto the deck.

"AST Damico just got one of them to the forty-seven," the pilot reported to Comms at Group Astoria.

"That's the guy I was really worried about," I said.

The man was lying on his back on the deck, but whether or not he was still alive, I wasn't sure. I kept the boat steady, rocking with the swell, feathering the throttles, trying to jog in place for the swimmer. As we were picking up the second guy off the boat, I heard one of my crew behind me saying, "What should I do? What should I do? I don't know what to do here."

I pivoted the boat again to face the waves and looked back over my shoulder. The man on the deck was foaming from the mouth, convulsing, then lying still, then convulsing again. Another set of waves was coming.

"Just do what you have to do," I said.

"I don't think he's conscious," he said.

"Is he breathing?" I asked.

"I don't think so," was the answer.

I radioed the pilot on the helicopter.

"He could be breathing," the pilot said. "Probably just tired, drained. A lot of them in the water give up like that."

"Roger that," I said.

A few minutes later the man's condition hadn't improved.

"Is he conscious at all?" the pilot asked over the radio.

"Negative. He's foaming at the mouth. No pulse," was my response.

"Is it foam or is he spitting out water?" he wanted to know.

"Foam," I said.

"Has CPR been administered?" the pilot asked.

"Negative. Not at this time," I said.

"What do you mean? You don't have anyone on board that has CPR qual?" The pilot sounded impatient. I understood why, but my crew couldn't do any more than they already were.

"We all are. We're kind of busy here," I said.

The capsized boat took another break and I heard more splitting at the bow. I circled around to the other side and turned our boat sideways, perpendicular to the oncoming waves, to block the capsized boat from taking more breaks.

"You want us to come get him with the basket," the pilot said, "or do you want to do more of what you're doing?"

"Negative," I said. "Not here. It's too big. We can't do a hoist; it's way too rough." The waves were lifting us up fifteen feet or more and nothing was stable. It would've been impossible to transfer a body from boat to air without someone, probably a member of my crew, getting seriously injured in the process. We couldn't afford that. We needed to wait and find calmer waters. Rule number one for a search-and-rescuer: Do not become part of your own case.

"Okay," the pilot said. "Looks like you've got it under control." And a moment later: "Oh man, this is intense. Big wave coming, big wave coming!"

A set of four waves was approaching us, whitecapping. The waves were sloughing rather than curling and breaking, so I wasn't worried about rolling the boat. I rotated the boat to port so the bow would take the brunt of the wave, protecting the crew on the deck.

"Two-four-eight, what is the status?" asked Comms at Group Astoria.

There were two others still in the water, but we had two of the four passengers on board the lifeboat. The first man who was foaming at the mouth was still on the deck; the other man was in the cabin. The second man seemed to be okay, responsive, no need for emergency treatment. The man on the deck, however, needed medical attention, and he needed it immediately. There wasn't much we could do for him, not at this point.

Beyond administering first aid and CPR, we weren't fully qualified to do much more. Because of the boat's thrashing motion and trying to get the others aboard, my crewmembers were not able to perform the necessary rounds of compressions.

The man was unresponsive. He was dying, I knew that now.

I was looking over my right shoulder, checking for waves, then back over my left shoulder to check on the capsized boat, and then, looking at the man, asking Giles for updates.

"He's not doing so well," he said.

"Two-four-eight, what is your status?" Astoria wanted to know.

"We have one person on board who needs immediate medical attention," I said into the radio.

"Is that first guy moving?" the pilot came in.

"Negative," I said. "Someone needs to call EMS."

Yes, the man was dying and, yes, he needed medical attention, but my hands were tied. I couldn't leave the others in the water, with the capsized boat beginning to break up, and we also couldn't transfer the first man to the helicopter here. That's when I made a decision. It might not have been the right one, but it was mine to make and I made it, with the full belief that it was the correct option, and that it couldn't have been done any differently or any better. I decided not to risk any more lives than necessary.

Things happen swiftly on a case and your instincts kick in. You don't have time to run through every single possibility, every possible action and reaction and consequence. I radioed the pilot, then Group Astoria, then Beach Command. I told them we were going to hold position until the rest of the passengers were on board, then find calmer waters where we would transfer the first guy to the helicopter, along with anyone else who was severely injured.

"Roger," the pilot said.

"You want to back off a bit?" I asked. "Your rotor wash is blowing me away from the boat."

The pilot held his position. He didn't hear me or he didn't respond. I never liked helicopter pilots much, with very few exceptions. They never seemed to understand what it was like, the sheer intensity of being down there, in the waves, in the thick of it. They got to sit up in their cockpits and watch from a safe distance. They didn't seem to understand what we were dealing with down in the water.

"I think he might be history," the pilot said, about the man foaming at the mouth.

"See if you can get a video of this," he said, talking to his flight crew. "This is crazy."

We picked up the other two passengers. One of them had a broken wrist, maybe, but other than that, they were fine. When we tried to pick up the rescue swimmer he started swimming in the other direction. We were getting pushed dangerously close to the jetty and I wanted to get moving. I wanted to get out of there.

"Take my swimmer with you. Grab my swimmer," the pilot said.

"You want to back off?" I said. "Your swimmer is unresponsive."

"Fucking rescue swimmer," Warren said.

As I mentioned, this case got a lot of media hype, mainly because a rescue swimmer was dispatched to the scene. Rescue swimmers tend to get all the credit in the Coast Guard, in the movies, in the press, in the media, and it's not completely undeserved. They are at peak physical condition, and there are simply not that many people who can do what they do on a daily basis. But they also have a reputation for arrogance, despite the fact that there are fewer qualified surfmen in the Coast Guard than qualified swimmers, and the process of becoming a surfman is a lot more rigorous. There are a lot of intricacies involved in learning to operate a boat and maneuver and negotiate that boat through heavy swell while also managing a crew and maintaining radio contact with the station and with other boats. There are simply a hundred things happening all at once, so you have to be able to make decisions, quickly and assertively, without second-guessing yourself or your crew.

The helicopter picked up their swimmer and I started making my way due west, out of the surf zone.

I radioed Beach Command. "Once I get out of the surf zone, we are going to try and hoist the most severely injured," I said. "It's one adult male, approximate age sixty-five. Took a lot of water into his lungs, it looks like. The three other passengers seem to be okay. But we need EMS at the dock as soon as possible."

"I understand you have all four victims out of the water," they said.

"Roger that," I said. "I'm headed due west to get out of this lump."

I told Warren to put the other three men in the survivors' compartment, below the cabin. He gave them blankets and told them to hold tight. It was going to be a rough few minutes. When he got back up to the helm, he told me they were all puking up gray water.

"They good other than that?" I said.

"Yeah," he said. "Just banged up a bit. Maybe a broken arm and some sprained wrists. Nothing serious."

"How's the first guy doing?"

Warren shook his head. "It doesn't look good," he said.

It took us maybe five minutes heading west, about a mile or so, to find a decent spot for the helicopter to transfer. The swell was still fifteen feet, but the waves weren't breaking on top of us anymore. During our training, we used to practice these kinds of hoists all the time with a dummy named Oscar, but never in surf like this. I told Warren and Wallace to head down to the deck and start preparing for a hoist, clearing the deck of the injured passenger and any debris.

"What's your plan?" the pilot asked. "You still want to hoist this guy?"

"Yeah," I said. "He has zero pulse and is still foaming at the mouth. I'd like to get in some calmer waters, but it doesn't look much better than this anywhere else. Just give me a couple more minutes and we'll hoist this guy."

"Roger. You going to be able to put him in a basket?"

"We'll find out in a second," I said.

"Okay. Roger that. We will give you a trail line and a basket."

"Just keep an eye out for swells in front of us," I said. "We will just maintain this same course and speed."

"Roger," said the pilot. "You keep going. We'll form on you."

We were doing six knots, heading on a straight line, south by southwest.

"Here come some big waves," the pilot said.

A set was forming a hundred yards away, moving quickly.

"I see it," I said.

"Here comes another one," the pilot said.

The radio crackled.

"Big wave!" the pilot said. "Big wave! Big wave!"

I told the crew to clip into their surf belts and the passengers to brace themselves in the compartment. We hit the waves, one after another, and each felt like we were running into a brick wall. Once we were over the last wave, there was a brief lull in the swell. This was our opening.

"All right," I radioed. "The deck is clear. We're ready to go whenever you are. Let's try to do this quickly."

"Roger. We're coming in for pickup. Can you ease back on the throttles?" asked the pilot.

I slowed down, cruising at a speed of five knots, just fast enough to roll over the sloughing breakers, the boat going up and down, up and down. The helicopter lowered itself, inch by inch, until it was above the stern, hovering thirty feet over us. The rhythmic pounding of the rotors, like a wall of sound, was almost all I could hear, mixed with faint yelling. The helicopter crew dropped the trail line with the basket and my crew worked quickly.

Warren secured the basket to the boat while Wallace and Giles lifted the man's body into the basket and secured it, all while we were hitting breakers. I turned to look over my shoulder. Warren gave me the thumbs-up, mouthing the words, "Ready to go."

I got back on the radio and alerted the flight team who started hoisting the basket up on the trail line. Wallace and Giles steadied it as it left the deck to keep it from swinging like a pendulum.

"All right," the pilot said. "We got him."

I turned around again. The man in the basket was suspended in the air, his body limp, his arms and legs dangling over the sides. I knew then that there was little chance of him surviving at this point. We had taken too long in retrieving the rest of the passengers from the water and the man had gone too long without medical treatment.

"He's secured in the cabin," the pilot said.

"Roger," I said.

"No pulse. He's not breathing. We're going to take him back to the volunteer beach command. You boys have a safe drive back."

"Roger," I said.

I turned the boat around, then radioed the Cape Watchtower. "We are headed back to the station now. We need EMS ready to go. Our ETA is roughly fifteen minutes," I said.

We tied up to the docks and a medical crew came on board to address the injuries of the three other survivors, which included a broken arm and a leg wound. The crew and I walked everyone out onto the dock. Huddled in gray blankets, I could see the relief in their faces once they set foot on dry land. A number of people had already begun to gather at the station: family, friends, police officers, firemen, EMTs. I was asked to do an interview by the local newspaper. I don't remember anything I said. There was nothing to say. The case wasn't a success. The man who was flown to Astoria was pronounced dead within the hour. It isn't a case I am particularly proud of, or one I like thinking about much. Courtney saved the news clippings that came out a couple days later, but I never read them.

"Great job," the CO said. "That was an incredible job." He came up from behind me and patted me on the back. "I thought you were definitely going to roll the boat. But you didn't. Well done. That was just amazing what you did out there." He reached out and shook my hand.

I tried to explain to him that these new 47s were designed to stand in sloughing breaks—that you don't have to fully square the boat to the waves. You will roll a bit, but not all the way.

"Sure," he said. "That makes sense. Great job, anyways."

He left to shake hands and talk to the reporters.

I dried off, changed back into my uniform, and went back to my office to fill out a report.

Within an hour, I got a phone call from the pilot stationed out of Group Astoria. His name was Josh Eliot. We weren't friends, but we had known each other for a couple years. We'd trained together and had worked on a handful of cases before, but never one like this. He told me the man had died. The news didn't come as a shock to me. I knew it before he told me.

We talked about the case for a while. It turned out that the four people on the boat were a family, two sons, a father, and a grandfather. The grandfather was the one who got swept off the boat and drowned. There was a long pause on the phone after he told me, as if he were expecting me to say something in response. Then, to break the silence, he asked me if I thought there was anything we could have done differently. It was an age-old question, something we'd asked ourselves before on previous cases, and something we'd ask ourselves years later. But it was a useless question.

"Do you think there was something we missed?" he asked.

"I don't know," I said. "I don't think so. We did everything we could."

Even now I don't know if that's true or if I was just lying to myself. Even now I haven't yet finished sorting it all out. My memory is blurred and vague and the events of the case come to me in flashes like rapid-fire images that make it difficult to see clearly, to see if there was something we messed up. I think sometimes that if we had responded more quickly, if we had communicated more clearly, if we had tried to hoist the man off immediately—maybe then he would have had a better chance.

Both of us knew it was pointless to play this game, asking ourselves these questions, sorting out all the hypotheticals, laying out all the contingencies, but we indulged ourselves just the same, if only to feel better about the roles we'd played in it. Sometimes I forgive myself for it all, other times I don't. When I am going about the ordinary hours of daily life, I try not to think about it, try not to let it consume me, though every now and then, the thought of it comes out of nowhere and hits me like a hammer. I stagger and have to sit down. Sometimes I hear the distant sound of rotor blades and I suddenly, like a vision, see the man being lifted up into a pale gray sky, his head bent to the side, his arms spread wide, as if embracing the air. I watch him ascend, slowly, slowly into the sky, until he disappears into the cabin of the helicopter.

After about an hour or so, Josh and I said our good-byes and I hung up the phone. We would talk about this case again a few months later. We kind of became friends. Once or twice a year, we went over this case, rehashing old details, asking ourselves the same questions. It was five or six years before we stopped talking about it. And it was even longer before I talked about it with anyone else.

Later that evening, news reporters from towns farther south were in Astoria interviewing the pilot and the rescue swimmer, and they asked to speak to me. I agreed to do one interview and that would be it. I always had a hard time interviewing directly after a case. My adrenaline was through the roof. I had a hard time looking at the cameras, looking directly at people or making eye contact, because I felt I was being scrutinized and my actions questioned. I didn't like the attention from people I didn't know, so I drove across the bridge to Astoria to do the interview and then drove back across the bridge to be with my family.

I am not ungrateful for the recognition or the commendations of heroism from my peers or the general public, but the attention wore on me.

Just when things seemed to be getting back to normal, I received an award from the Association for Rescue at Sea (AFRAS) for what was dubbed the Peacock Spit Case. I shook the hands of Transportation Secretary Norman Mineta and Congressman Sam Farr as I received the award, for my "dedication, judgment, and devotion to duty," which was "directly responsible for the successful rescue of three lives."

But all I heard was the number "three," not "four."

Afterward, strangers approached me to shake my hand. I nodded and smiled and said thank you. Not all of them knew there was another man, a fourth life that was not being acknowledged. I was grateful for the recognition, but I also knew it wasn't the whole story. In my eyes it wasn't a successful case or something I could be proud of. As I saw it, unless I'd rescued everyone involved, it was difficult to think of it as anything other than a failed mission.

The military holds sacred the belief in sacrifice, which involves giving one life to save others. But we do not talk about it as such; we use the language of heroism and honor. In the months and years following the Peacock Spit rescue, this thought crept into my bones, this idea of sacrifice—whether or not my decisions and actions that day led to the sacrifice of one man for the lives of three others. Did I know this? Was I aware of the implications of my choices? Were they conscious decisions? I wish I could say. I have run through the details of the case a thousand times, and I simply do not know anymore.

I paced around the house most of the night after the rescue. When I tried to go to bed, Courtney woke up. She asked me if I was okay, and I told her I was, though that wasn't true. She held me and she fell back asleep.

I stared up at the spinning ceiling fan, then closed my eyes and laid my head on the pillow. I kept seeing the man's lifeless body on the deck, foaming at the mouth. I was still hearing the pilot's voice coming in over the radio.

Is he conscious?

Is he breathing?

Is he alive?

Big wave coming! Big wave coming!

Boom! Boom! Boom!

Chapter Eleven

The Association for Rescue at Sea

PETTY OFFICER BM1 SAM KINSEY WAS A TALL MAN, WITH A SQUARISH head and an athletic build, who wore his brown hair cut close to the scalp. He walked with his shoulders slumped, which made him look shorter than he was. I always thought his demeanor was strangely sad. He was a qualified surfman out of Station Cape Disappointment, three years into his tour, when I was just working my way through qualifications in 1999.

Kinsey made an impression on me because he was awarded the gold medal from AFRAS, one of the highest honors for search-and-rescuers at the time I was becoming a surfman. His big rescue happened in the middle of the night, in late winter, in Clatsop Spit. The Spit is a giant sandbar north of the South Jetty, between the jetties and the buoy. It was formed thousands of years ago by sediment carried to the coast by the river's flow and it was shaped by the wind and waves until a broad sandy plain was formed. The Spit acts as one side of the funnel where the river meets the ocean, intensifying the water's turbulence.

Clatsop was where Kinsey responded to a capsized boat that was being pushed into the rocks one evening. The waves weren't too big or too unmanageable, but by the time he and his crew got to the scene, the boat had turned over and was sinking quickly. There was a kid and his dad on board who had been fishing a couple hours earlier before the weather turned. They were trapped in the cabin of the capsized boat.

Kinsey's crew got the dad off the boat, but the boy was trapped in an air pocket in the enclosed bridge and they couldn't get to him. The boat sank and the boy drowned. His body was picked up a couple days later, washed up onshore not too far away.

I thought of Kinsey's case often in the weeks and months after my Peacock Spit case. There were similarities between them, from both cases getting a lot of attention in the press, news coverage in print and on television, to both becoming a big deal among the search-and-rescue community. Although there was a lot of talk about Kinsey from station to station along the coast of the Pacific Northwest, I remember that he never spoke about it, not a single word, and I respected him for that. To him, I guess it was just another failed case, but one that was made memorable by all the attention it got and the accolades he received. Despite the attention I'm sure Kinsey couldn't stop thinking of the boy he couldn't rescue, the one who drowned, and I knew exactly how he felt. I couldn't stop thinking of the man *I* couldn't rescue, the one *I* let drown.

The aftermath of the Peacock Spit case was unexpected. I felt lost, as if I were sleepwalking. I wandered around my house and the station, not sure about directions, north, south, east, and west, moving robotically, not sure where my feet were taking me sometimes. The connection between my brain and my body was broken. I had trouble doing the simplest of tasks. I groped for my equipment, my helmet, and my uniform in the mornings. I couldn't sit still for more than ten minutes. When I ran in the forest my feet felt like they were balls of lead attached to cement cylinders. I swallowed whatever it was that was bitter and rising in my stomach and boarded the Bar boat every morning. In my office I stared out the window at the gulls diving for chum thrown by fishermen in the shallows. I felt cut off, severed from something I didn't know how to talk about. I'm sure Courtney and the kids could tell something was wrong, but I couldn't talk about it with them.

The media attention wore off in a couple months, but just in time for a one-page letter to arrive in the mail from someone in Washington, DC. It said I would receive the same award as Kinsey had gotten three years earlier, the AFRAS gold medal. I read it in my office in the boathouse where we did maintenance work. I sank down in my chair and stared out the window. A stack of paperwork was piling up at the edge of my desk, the trash bin needed to be emptied, and maintenance orders needed to be submitted. I was just beginning to get back into a healthy, comfortable routine, just beginning to push away thoughts of the case, just starting to forget about it and move on when the letter came.

I would accept the award a year later.

In November 2002 Courtney and I traveled to our nation's capital. Washington, DC felt like Mars to Courtney and me. We arrived a day before the award ceremony and walked for hours, sightseeing. The scale and busyness of the city was foreign and the frenzied pace helped to keep me from thinking too much about the ceremony I'd be part of, or the significance of the Peacock Spit case. Neither of us had been to Washington before, so on the first day we went to the Smithsonian and the Korean War Veterans Memorial. We walked past the Library of Congress, the White House, the Capitol building, and the Lincoln Memorial. All of the pavement and noise and man-made features were a jarring contrast with tiny Ilwaco, its tall evergreens and small bait shops and fishing boats and logging trucks. I had a hard time adjusting to it all.

My mind was swimming as we experienced skyscrapers, people everywhere in expensive suits, homeless people, and the sounds of traffic: horns honking and brakes screeching and people yelling out their windows. It seemed like everywhere we went there were helicopters hovering overhead and police officers on every street corner. It was overwhelming. Everywhere we went I felt conspicuous, as if we were being watched.

We went back to the hotel and ate burgers at the restaurant in the hotel lobby and relaxed at the bar. On television the Packers were dueling it out with the Saints.

Courtney went to bed before me. I stood at the window and stared out at the streetlights and the headlights of cars coming and going. It was raining and it was late. Courtney woke up when I got into bed.

"You nervous?" she said.

"No," I said. "Not really. Just tired."

"You have your speech ready?"

"Yeah."

"It'll be fine," she said. "Tomorrow will be great."

"Yeah," I said. "I know."

"I'm glad you decided to accept the award. I think it'll be great for you."

"Yeah," I said. "I know."

She smiled at me the way she does when she's tired and happy. She kissed me on the forehead, then turned back over and fell asleep. I was exhausted, but I couldn't sleep much that night. I stood at the window again to look out at the streets. The traffic had dispersed. Only a few homeless men and late-night drunks stumbled down the empty streets. I thought about those nights in the cold Alaska ports, moving from bar to bar, drunk and young and in love. I remembered all those months on the *Sherman*, away from Courtney, working on cleanup crews and maintenance crews and chipping paint off the sides of the boat. I remembered those early months of fatherhood, of moving to Ilwaco. I remembered feeling helpless, arriving at edge of the Pacific, at the mouth of the Columbia River, unaware what the future held. I remembered staring at those famous waters for the first time, in complete awe, watching those giant broad-faced waves spitting and churning and knuckle-slapping, tearing each other to pieces.

It had been a long time, but now I was scared again. No part of me wanted to go to the ceremony to accept the award and the medal. I didn't want to shake the hands of people who believed I was some kind of hero. I stayed up all night, feeling uneasy. Making it worse was standing there and staring out the window at the city lights and not seeing an ocean in any direction.

The ceremony was held in an office near the White House the following day. My dad, my uncle Joey, Courtney, and I went to a bar around the corner for a couple of beers before heading over there. My dad and uncle had flown down from New York and met us downtown, where I told them if I was going to do this I needed to get a few drinks into me, and they were happy to oblige. It was before noon and the bar was empty, dimly lit, and best of all, quiet.

My uncle and I started talking and playing catch-up. I hadn't seen him or talked to him in several years. He was short and stocky and barrel-chested and ate a ton, and it seemed not much had changed. When I was younger I visited him and my dad's side of the family in Queens every summer. He took me all around Manhattan, to the Statue of Liberty and to the top of the World Trade Center, and he used to take me to the horse races at the Aqueduct. We reminisced about all of that and more and talked about our kids and work. We laughed and made jokes and told stories of the past few years. We ordered another round.

Before we went into the ceremony, Courtney pulled me aside.

"Just relax," she said. "It'll be fine."

I smiled at her, a little drunk.

"This is nothing," she said. "You've done way harder things than this."

I wasn't sure that I had.

The ceremony was attended by twenty AFRAS members and the five recipients of the awards, as well as friends and family. There was a buffet-style spread of food, an open bar. My uncle and I tended in that direction.

"Nice duds, by the way," my uncle said about my bravo dress blue uniform, which consisted of blue wool pants and a white Air Force–style collared shirt, where my ribbons were pinned. Most of those in attendance were highly decorated officers, commanders and chiefs, with all colors of ribbons and medals and pendants fastened to their chests. I had only been in the Coast Guard for six years and had two commendation medals, one achievement medal, and a letter of commendation, which was respectable. But compared to some of the others in uniform, mine looked meager and pitiful.

At the buffet, I looked down at all the food and kept seeing dismembered body parts. That made it hard to fill a plate.

"I'm starving," my uncle said.

"I'm going to be at the bar," I said.

Seeing as the drinks were free, I had a couple beers to calm my nerves a bit. The nervousness was not so much anticipation as unease. I have never liked functions like this, especially award ceremonies. Among those in attendance were Secretary of Transportation Norman Mineta, Vice Admiral Thomas Collins, Admiral James Gracey, and Congressman Sam Farr. The vice admiral came over to where I was at the bar when Courtney and my dad and uncle were sitting at a table near the back of the room. Almost everyone in the Coast Guard knew his name, as he was on the short list to become the next commandant, and would get promoted to admiral upon assuming office. He later became an integral part of the Coast Guard's absorption into Homeland Security after the attacks on 9/11. He oversaw, for instance, the redirection of over fifty cutters from fisheries missions or counter-drug enforcement to major ports in the country, like New York, Boston, and Los Angeles. He shook my hand and we exchanged pleasantries.

"Can I get you a drink, son?" he asked.

"Yeah, I'll take another one," I said. "Heineken is fine."

He ordered a couple beers from the bartender.

"Thanks," I said.

He took a sip and set his glass down on the countertop.

"That was good work you did out there," he said.

I felt myself wince.

"Thanks," I said.

"I wanted to personally congratulate you and thank you for your service."

I felt myself wince again.

"Thank you."

I guess I didn't know what else to say.

"The search-and-rescue work you boys do out there is just amazing. Absolutely incredible."

"Thank you. We were just doing our jobs."

"The way I see it," he said, "is not many people can do your job."

"I guess so," I said.

"See, there you have it," he said. "Your kind, you're a special breed." Then he said, "Well, I got to go get ready. It was nice meeting you in person. Thanks for the drink."

He finished his beer and we shook hands again and he left.

The ceremony started soon after that. I took my seat at the back of the room with my family around a wooden table with a white tablecloth. I drank another beer. Vice Admiral Collins walked up to the podium at the front of the room and began to speak about the history of AFRAS. He spoke of the amount of training and dedication and work required by search-and-rescuers, and some of the notable past recipients. He used words like *selflessness* and *courage*, *honor* and *heroism*, but I had forgotten what some of those words meant.

The first award given that year was a silver medal, which was always given to a member of the Auxiliary, the civilian unit within the Coast Guard reserves whose primary function is to assist in search and rescue and boating safety patrols, pretty much everything except law enforcement.

The honoree for the Auxiliary award was Henry "Cleve" Chandler, who was fishing at Lake Tangipahoa in Mississippi when a Plymouth minivan slid down an embankment and into the lake. Diving into the water, Chandler arrived at the passenger's window and saw an elderly couple inside, frozen in terror. He tried to instruct them on what to do but they were unresponsive. Chandler swam back to the fishing boat, got a life jacket, and put it on the driver. He then assisted the man from the minivan, which was taking on water quickly. As the man was pulled out the van sank several feet, disappearing from sight, taking the woman in the passenger seat and Chandler with it. Chandler swam back up to the surface to get a breath of air then dove back down again. Witnesses reported he was underwater for several minutes before he came back up with the woman, who was semiconscious. Both passengers recovered fully within the next few days, thanks in large part to Chandler's quick and selfless actions.

After the description of Chandler's rescue was read there was a brief silence, followed by applause. The tall, balding man stepped up and accepted his medal. He gave a short speech, then went back to his table and sat down to more applause.

Next, the vice admiral awarded the AMVER plaque to the captain and crew of a Norwegian-flagged freighter, the M/V *Tampa*, for a rescue of more than four hundred survivors. They were somewhere in the Indian Ocean when they received a distress alert from an overloaded twenty-meter wooden boat with a disabled engine that was taking on water. The *Tampa* captain and master altered their course, made visual contact, and observed that most of the passengers were belowdecks. If the passengers had been above the waterline the boat might have capsized.

The captain maneuvered the *Tampa* to provide shelter, a lee, for the distressed vessel, and backed down alongside it. Using the main engine and forward and aft thrusters, he brought his vessel parallel to the wooden boat without further endangering its precarious situation. One at a time the passengers were moved up the ship's accommodation ladder. Three crewmen took turns lifting each person from the boat onto the ladder and onto the freighter. "The final count of all survivors was four hundred and thirty-eight in total," the vice admiral said. "Three hundred sixty-nine men, twenty-six women, forty-three children." More applause.

Then it was our turn.

The vice admiral began: "Petty Officer D'Amelio is cited for outstanding achievement while serving as surfman on board Coast Guard Motor Lifeboat 47248 on the afternoon of September 2, 2001, for his actions in the rescue of four persons ejected from their twenty-two-foot recreational fishing boat by a twenty-foot wave in the vicinity of Peacock Spit at the mouth of the Columbia River . . ."

As the vice admiral recounted the case I could see all of it happening again. Certain images flashed rapidly through my head: the capsized boat being shattered by waves, the waves washing the man off the boat, the man floating facedown in the water, then foaming at the mouth on the deck. I couldn't help but think that they had gotten it all wrong. It should've read the "rescue of three persons," because only three had been successfully rescued.

The vice admiral continued. "[U]pon turning north of the jetty, Petty Officer D'Amelio encountered fifteen- to eighteen-foot breaking surf with occasional wave crests over twenty feet high. Arriving on scene, the crew sighted four people clinging to the overturned vessel. Petty Officer D'Amelio skillfully maneuvered the lifeboat through the breaking surf to within two hundred yards of the overturned vessel. To prevent the lifeboat from being rolled by the plunging breakers, he squared the bow into the surf while attempting to back the lifeboat to the survivors.

"Skillfully contending with the mammoth surf, Petty Officer D'Amelio directed his crew in retrieving the survivors. Teaming with Coast Guard Helicopter 6008, he calmly and expertly maneuvered the lifeboat near the capsized boat while a rescue swimmer from the helicopter swam the survivors to his crew.

"After retrieving all four survivors, Petty Officer D'Amelio quickly sought calmer water where he and his crew more closely evaluated the survivors' conditions. Determining one survivor needed immediate medical attention, he quickly coordinated and directed the transfer of this individual to the waiting helicopter.

"Petty Officer D'Amelio's superb surfman skills and leadership in the most demanding of circumstances was directly responsible for the saving of three lives . . ."

Three lives, I was reminded again. Three lives, and not four, was all I heard.

"... and his dedication and judgment and devotion to duty are most heartily commended and are in keeping with the highest traditions of the US Coast Guard. Please join me in congratulating him today and all of his successes."

There was applause. I stood up and walked to the podium, a little bit buzzed. I shook hands with the congressman and the admirals and commanders and was given the certificate, a small amount of money, and the medal. I had a speech rehearsed. I had written and rewritten it several times over the past month and it hadn't improved. I had read it out loud in front of the mirror, trying on different inflections and facial expressions. It was a simple speech, maybe overly modest. I stumbled through it. It deflected a lot of the attention and recognition. By most standards it was pretty uninspiring.

"Thank you," I said. "Thank you to the Association and to the admiral and vice admiral and to everyone in attendance. This is a real honor for me and my wife and my family. But really, I had the easy job. My crew and those at the station that worked on the case deserve the real recognition. They had the hard job. All I did was drive the boat." I paused for another short burst of applause.

When I walked back to my seat and sat down, my hands were trembling. Courtney placed her hand on my shoulder, then looked at me and winked, and all the storms inside me calmed.

The rescue swimmer AST Alan Damico was announced and awarded the same medal and certificate after me. Vice Admiral Collins made a point of saying that this was the first time the medal had been given to two members of the Coast Guard in the same year, and for the same case. I knew Alan. Our paths had crossed on several other cases in the past, although we had never really talked about any of them before, never debriefed. We weren't friends, but I respected him and his work. His job was to pull the bodies out of the water, dead or alive, and I knew he had seen his fair share of blood and gore. Like me, he knew that this award didn't change anything—that the fourth man we'd rescued was dead, and we couldn't go back and do things differently if we wanted to.

There was uneasiness gathered in his shoulders, in the way he walked, when he stepped up to the podium to accept the award. He looked around the room for a moment, as if he were trying to take its measure, to size it up. The vice admiral asked if he'd like to say a few words. There was a long pause. Traditionally, most who accept the award give a speech, but it looked like he hadn't prepared one. It looked like he was trying to figure it out on the spot, what he wanted to say next, or at least the precise wording of it. Finally, he turned to the vice admiral and said, "No." Then he exited, stage left.

The weekend after we got back from DC, Courtney and I took the kids out for a day at the beach. I want to record a moment from that day here, before I forget it. We were down by the water collecting seashells and polished stones and sea glass, which Courtney later put in a jar and set on the dining room table. Down the beach, a wind had blown the picnic blanket Courtney had brought for the picnic she packed. Around noon, the weather took a turn and a storm blew in from offshore and scattered rain over the ocean and hillsides. By the time we got to the car to drive home, everyone was soaked from head to foot, and we all came down with a cold later that week. I took time off work and stayed home, and for a few days none of us left the house.

Here's another good memory I want to preserve. One Sunday, around the time they were four and two years old, I took Taylor and Matthew to fish off the end of the pier, where the Coast Guard station casts its long shadow across the deck. We had been fishing out here for the better half of the morning, with nothing to show for it. Out past the end of the dock, the sea lions swam through the wreckage of an old boat and the pelicans dove headlong into the waves. It was one of those weird days in early winter when the sun never stops shining and yet the rain comes down in soft sheets. The fishermen just ignore it, pretending like it's not raining at all. On this day their fishing rods were fastened to metal hooks in the chewed-up railing, bending under the weight of a fish. They had been here throwing their lines out into the dark cove before daybreak, catching rockfish and perch and the occasional halibut. The fish were usually too small to keep, but the men threw them into iceboxes anyway, the fish gasping for water.

A couple of seagulls circled overhead, landing on the deck and strutting up and down the wooden railing, scrabbling for bits of bait. The pier shook under our feet as the waves rolled in off the sandbar and were obliterated against the pilings. Several years before, a child had gone missing and was found washed up onshore, not far from here, his body tangled in seaweed. The night before I'd had a dream about a man found buried in the sand beneath a wharf. He was wearing a black coat and a pair of shiny black boots. His clothes were wet. Thousands of seashells surrounded him on the shore.

Chapter Twelve

Last Tow

THE WEATHER IN ILWACO CHANGED SO SWIFTLY. FROM YEAR TO YEAR, we passed through the seasons, tracking and following the ocean's patterns, the wind's patterns. Winters were always a hallucinatory season, one to be survived. When spring came the ocean calmed and the chinook began their run up the Columbia. Summers meant salmon season and summer vacationers, which meant we were busy. I have always enjoyed the ocean most in autumn, especially the early weeks of November. When the winds began to kick up again, the ocean's breakers crashing, the town emptied out, and once again the beaches were empty, with no human presence to spoil the natural beauty. Then, without mercy, came winter.

By the time our son Matthew was born I considered Ilwaco our new home. He was born in the middle of a cold winter, on January 24, 2000, the year before the towers fell, the beginning of a new century, a new and terrifying era. I wonder sometimes what it must be like for my kids' generation, not knowing a world where it hadn't happened.

Before she gave birth to Matthew, Courtney and I spent several weeks converting the back room of the house into the baby's room, with a crib, a changing table, a mobile hung from the ceiling, all furnishings left over from our first, Taylor. Taylor was already two years old, beginning to speak in full sentences, making small demands and showing her independence. She has always been the most independent of our three children, the one who needed the least guidance. Matthew was needier. He breastfed longer, took longer to potty-train, needed more attention day to day. He was born at the hospital in Astoria, across the Columbia River. I remember the day he was born it rained all through the night and into the morning, and in the afternoon the clouds broke.

Fatherhood never came easy to me; it was never as intuitive for me as driving a boat through heavy surf because there was so much more to consider, so much more time to second-guess myself. Damage to a boat could always be fixed. Damage to a child could live beneath the surface, slumbering, appearing only years later, irreparable. That was always my main worry, that as a parent I would make a mistake that could never be fixed.

I had a hard time with fatherhood from the beginning, when Taylor was a newborn. I wasn't much help in those early months. I came home from work and felt ineffectual. Courtney was either nursing or putting the baby to sleep or changing a diaper. I wanted to help her, to be of use, but I just felt completely unnecessary, like a soldier in limbo waiting for his next assignment. I tried to keep a confident attitude, but in truth I was terrified. For a while, I was even scared to hold the baby, imagining some defect or long-buried violence being shed from me and onto her. I doubted my ability to raise her without making a mess of things.

I learned to be a father over time, much like the way one becomes a grown-up.

It was around four a.m., the first morning after we'd brought Matthew home from the hospital. I had work in a couple hours. The house was cold and quiet. Taylor was asleep in her room, and Courtney was asleep in the nursing chair in the baby's room. The baby was asleep in the crib, though it wouldn't be for long. When I heard him crying I was in the living room, half-asleep on the couch. I went into the baby's room where Courtney was still sleeping, a blanket wrapped around her shoulders. I shook her awake and told her she should go to bed.

"I got this one," I said.

She refused at first, rubbing her eyes with the back of her hand, then finally relented and walked down the hallway to bed.

I picked Matthew up from the crib. He was curled into a ball, wailing, screaming so loud I was surprised it didn't wake any of the neighbors. I gave him a bottle and cradled him in the crook of my arm, pacing around the house. The night was clear and cold and quiet. Other than his wailing, all I could hear were the crickets in the backyard, the waves lapping at the shore, a light breeze coming and going.

Still holding Matthew I went out the back door, climbed down the bank, and removed my shoes and socks. The murky water of the river whirlpooled in the shallows. It was cold on my skin, and the chill of the air pricked at my skin. Sediment shifted between my feet, drifting away as I joggled the baby in my arms. He was quieting down now. In that silence it was almost as if I could hear the blood coursing through my veins, the same in his, and the steady rhythm of our heartbeats. His eyes were closed and he was cooing softly.

"It's going to be okay," I said, and pointed skyward to the North Star to give him his bearings.

My last long tow came in the summer of 2005 during the Halibut Derby. This was a recreational fishing contest held annually at the mouth of the Columbia River, offering cash prizes and trophies, picnics and barbecues, and it usually lasted all week. At the station, we worked around the clock, doing security, patrolling the waters, making sure all the fishermen had proper safety and boating equipment.

These were my last weeks at Cape Disappointment. Five months had passed since I'd asked for a transfer, to move south to the Coast Guard station on the Siuslaw River. Six months had passed since the case with the Russian girl who drowned by the North Head Lighthouse. Something intangible but real had changed in me after that case. I felt lost for a few months after the incident. Maybe the transfer would return my bearings, allow me to find my footing again. The timing seemed right because nothing else was lining up the way it should.

That day the Russian girl died was still fresh in my mind. I remembered it with such clarity—the rotor blades creating ripples along the surface of the water, kicking dust off the cliffs, the girl's screams, loud and insistent, then gradually quieting, the helicopter seeming to freeze above the ocean for an instant, as if a camera had clicked, and the girl's body in the basket, hanging, suspended in midair for several long moments, her red shoes bright against the milky blue sky. I remember something rising up from my stomach to the back of my throat. I saw myself, probably for the first time, as something small and terrified of the world, terrified for my children, my family, terrified for myself. I saw my armor of confidence and ability slowly falling away.

My last long haul was during the Halibut Derby, which typically coincides with the opening of tuna season every year. The tuna arrives off the coast of Oregon and Newport in large shoals in the mid- to late-summer months when the southern winds bring warm water north from Mexico and fishing boats flock to the area in droves.

One afternoon near the end of the 2005 contest we got a call from a tuna boat disabled seventy miles offshore. Most the other boats were already out on a case or doing safety patrol for the fishing derby. The only boat still tied up at the docks was the fifty-two-foot *Triumph*, a boat I had come to love, one I'd cleaned and painted and maintained for the past five years. I figured it might be my last time to drive this boat, so I volunteered for the tow. I got together a crew willing to take the nearly twenty-four-hour transit. When we finally got under way it was late in the afternoon and the halibut boats were already coming back into the docks.

The disabled boat was just within our area of responsibility, due west, but well out of range to make radio contact with the station. It took nearly eight hours to get there, all smooth sailing.

When we were alongside them, the captain was standing up on the helm, waving his cap to us. "Glad you guys found us," he yelled across the boats. "We've been stuck out here for a few hours now."

"What happened?" I yelled back.

"Not sure," he said. "Engine just stopped."

We tossed them the towline and they tied it to the bow of their boat. I radioed the captain and told him we were going to get going. We made about five turns on the tow bit and let out eight hundred feet of line. It was well past midnight by this time. Without any light pollution the sky was so clear and the stars so incredibly bright we could see the white smear of the Milky Way swept across the sky like the stroke of a paintbrush.

An hour later, I got a call over the radio from the captain.

"Hey, you mind if we try to fish as long as we're out here?" he asked. "You're going the perfect speed."

Ten years before, back in the old days of commercial fishing, something like that wouldn't have been a big deal. There were fewer rules then, less regulation. But we were in a legal gray area when it came to helping commercial fishermen fish. Since we were well out of radio range and no one would find out, I didn't see why not. None of the fishermen looked like they were going to say anything. Most of my house was already packed up in boxes, waiting for the movers. Courtney and I were planning for our new home in Florence, Oregon. We were leaving in less than six weeks.

"Sure," I said. "Why not?"

There were three other fishermen on the tuna boat and they all started letting their lures out. We made a deal that every time they got a fish on the line, they had to call it out as we drove through the night. They caught fish. We chatted over the radio. The stars wheeled across the sky and fell into the ocean beyond the horizon. The captain spoke with a thick Midwestern accent. He was from Wisconsin, he said, where he had worked on commercial fishing boats his whole life, since he was fourteen years old, fishing for whitefish and herring in Lake Michigan and Lake Superior. The last couple of years, he had worked up in Alaska during crab season, but had finally decided he couldn't stand the cold and moved further south.

The hours-long monotony of the tow and the calm water allowed us to take our minds off the business at hand, to chat and think and reminisce as the water passed beneath our boats.

"People complain about the weather here," he said, "but it's really not that bad. Try living in Wisconsin for a while. Or Alaska. That place will freeze your nuts off. I like it down here. The rain is a problem, but the fishing is as good as anywhere else. Say, you married?"

"Yeah," I said. "Almost ten years."

"That's impressive. You're talking to someone who's been divorced twice. You got any kids?"

"Yeah," I said. "I have a son and a daughter."

"Hey, me too," he said. "With my second wife. What a coincidence." Then he said, "Fish on."

"Guys sound like you're doing pretty well back there," I said.

"Yeah, not bad," he said.

"You guys make your quota?"

"Yeah. But I figured we could make some extra money this way," he said.

I laughed.

Then he said, "You're a father, so you know how it is. This is so much easier. Isn't it?"

"Yeah, I know what you mean," I replied.

My work had always been so much easier for me than fatherhood. There was something about putting my body in harm's way to make a living that was simpler than raising a child. There was only so much you had to think about out on the water: wave speed, wind speed, swell height. Back at home, I was attempting to raise two human beings, making mistakes, watching those mistakes manifest themselves, then second-guessing my decisions while simply hoping my child would grow into an adult one day. Basic instinct demands that a father's primary job is to protect his children from the violence of the world, but the actual process of raising a child is not as straightforward. I think that's what he meant.

"So how long you been in the Coast Guard?"

"It'll be ten years next year," I said.

"You going to stay on for another ten?"

"I think so," I said.

"So you like it then, I take it."

"Yeah," I said. "Well, not everything. Parts of it are good. Parts of it are not."

I wasn't sure if I had ever said this out loud to anyone, including Courtney and myself. Whatever reward I'd reaped from this job wasn't worth it anymore, I realized, but I was scared to leave it behind. I had spent the last six years becoming a surfman, using it as a way to measure my self-worth, to test my mettle against the water, against others, against my own limitations. It was only several months ago that I'd reached that horizon, found the edge of what I was capable of handling.

When someone died while I was out on a case, I always found it hard to mourn. It was necessary that I keep moving forward, never allow myself to get too sentimental about the dead. But it would be a mistake to say that the death of the Russian girl had nothing to do with how my idea of myself had changed after that. I understood that for most of my life I had mistaken fear for weakness; then I saw my real weakness begin to surface, and it was pride.

It has been difficult to forgive myself for what happened that day, and the process has taken years. Some days I can forgive myself and feel a little relief from the guilt of her death, but it never lasts very long.

Inevitably I end up thinking of her: frail-looking and lifeless. I think of all the people she could have been: a teacher, a gymnast, an astronaut or a painter. Maybe she was not so different from my own daughter. Her deafening cries remind me of how terrified she was, and how terrified I was. And eventually, I remember how I did nothing, and how for five minutes, I stood by and watched, allowed her to drown. That is the real story I want to tell: that I was angry, and that I was terrified. I'm not sure the rawness of my fear and terror will ever heal and stop hurting.

There was plenty of time to think about these things as we towed the tuna boat. The night passed steadily to the hum of the boat engine, until the darkened hills of the horizon were lit up all at once by a pallid flash of rosy light. We still had nine more hours before we'd be back at the station, and by then it would be well past noon. My crew was tired, taking shifts sleeping and standing watch. The morning star appeared over the hills in the east, then vanished. The sun rose, casting sharp blades of light across the surface of the water.

I listened to the wind above us, to the waves slapping the boat. The coastal hillsides in the distance seemed to glow phosphorescent in the morning light. A flock of pelicans flew overhead, vanishing to the south. I picked up the radio.

"This part is pretty good," I said.

"Yeah," the fishing captain said. "I roger that."

Then he said, "Fish on."

My very last tow was on the Fourth of July during my last month at the station. Transfer season was usually midsummer because kids were out of school. Most of the boats were fishing offshore that last summer I lived on the Cape. Similar to the Halibut Derby, the Fourth was a day full of drunk people fishing and driving boats. It was always a busy day. I volunteered to work the Fourth that year because it was my last.

In the evening there was still light on the horizon when we received a distress call from a tuna boat that was disabled at the northern boundary of our jurisdiction, about six miles offshore. I remember getting down to the docks as quickly as I could because it was dusk and the light was vanishing. I wanted to get out there before it got dark. The sky was gray and the water was gray, but it was warm and mild, and fog had been pouring in from offshore all day long as we picked up broken-down boats and drunk fishermen. We took one of the forty-seven-foot lifeboats, left the gates at the channel, turned the corner at the A Jetty, and exited the Bar. The captain of the tuna boat had given us his position.

The sun sank well beyond the horizon and night crossed the water, turning it dark, then darker still. The night wind picked up, but the water was still calm and flat, almost no swell at all. We were cruising along, listening to the thrum of the engine. I was feeling sentimental and sad and hopeful all at once, the noise from town slowly beginning to fade away until it was gone altogether, and there was only the boat skating steadily across the smooth surface of the ocean. There was no sound except the engine and the water slapping at the sides of the boat.

We were towing the tuna boat back to Ilwaco when the fog and the clouds lifted. Just when we rounded the tip of the jetty we heard a loud concussive boom, then another one. The shock of it reverberated in the boat, startling me. Then I saw a flare snake its way up into the sky, leaving behind a trail of white light before exploding into hundreds of sparks. Then another one went up. Then another and another. The entire shoreline up and down the coast was lit up by fireworks, and as the night wore on the fireworks got bigger and more elaborate, with fountains of color and light showering the ocean, and the air sweet with the tangy smell of smoke and gunpowder.

I radioed the captain on the tuna boat and together we decided to slow down and watch the show. We snuck in along the beach and I set the Fathometer to keep us in twenty feet of water so we could just sit back and watch. No one was in a rush to get home because we had front-row seats. We had seen fireworks before, but never like this, never such a panoramic view. When one went off, it seemed like fifty others were going off, all of them curling and twisting and spiraling, crackling and machine-gun popping, showering the ocean with light. Every member of my crew and the crew on the tuna boat was on deck with their heads tilted up, staring at the sky. No one moved for several minutes, entranced by the spectacle.

I lost track of time. We might have been out there for an hour, maybe two. Others had the same idea, as hundreds of fishing boats were still out on the Bar by the time we left, their shadows lit up every now and then by the brilliance of the colorful lights.

CHAPTER THIRTEEN

Farewell

THREE MONTHS BEFORE I TRANSFERRED TO FLORENCE, OREGON, Courtney and I bought our first house. We met with several real estate agents before we found someone we liked, a fifty-something retired navy guy. He showed us a house on a quiet back road along the Siuslaw River, only a mile from town. It was small, with three bedrooms and two bathrooms and an olive-green paint job. When we moved in it took me three days with a backhoe to clear out the tree roots, the brush, the bushes and thorns tangled in the backyard, and we never got around to repainting it, but the house was in a good school district and a new neighborhood right next to the fire and police stations. We took out a loan from the bank, made a bid, and put down a deposit. While the house was in escrow, we drove back up to Ilwaco and started packing up our home there. It was summer, 2005.

Ilwaco was the place we'd lived the longest. It was where we'd started our family, met some lifelong friends, where Courtney became a mother, where we watched our children speak their first words and take their first steps. It was also where I discovered myself in a trade, where I tested myself against the waters of chaos and came out scarred and bruised and beaten. I'd been beaten but emerged alive and breathing. Still, I was terrified to leave it all behind.

The Coast Guard hired us a moving company, one of the perks of working for the government. They did it all: They came to see how much stuff we had and provided all the supplies and packed up our belongings in boxes and duffel bags and left them in the corner of the living room, stacked to the ceiling. The pile was overwhelming: boxes of clothes and sports equipment, computers and TVs and stereo equipment, beds and sofas and tables and chairs, boxes of kitchenware and linens and framed pictures and bathroom toiletries. I was relieved not to have to think about any of it. It was hard enough to see it all packed up in boxes. Later the movers came to the house, loaded up a truck, and unloaded everything into our new house in Florence.

Before we left, the station threw a big farewell party for everyone who was moving on, transferring to another unit. There was a big party every year, always in late July, because the summertime was transfer season, which meant good-byes and farewells. But it also meant new towns, new lives, new friends, new families, new joys and trials and tribulations. We bought a couple of kegs and went out to the gazebo by the shore and barbecued clams, mussels, salmon, halibut, crab, and oysters. The clouds were benevolent that day, the sunlight incandescent. Though we generally took any excuse we could find to get together and eat and drink, these parties always seemed a rare and special occasion, probably because they signified change, for the station and for us.

When I was loading a second helping of food on my plate I was talking with Kaleb, who was on grill duty, watching flames searing tuna steaks and cooking a rack of mussels. He was staying on for another year, maybe two, and would be taking over some of my duties. I had some idea that we might have a personal talk but instead we just shared a beer and talked about fishing. The season had been a good one for salmon and steelhead, better than previous years, which meant it was a busy season for the Coast Guard. Before fall, Kaleb said he was planning on taking a hunting trip up north, for elk.

We had worked together for four years, sharing innumerable meals and working countless cases. We had spent Christmases and Thanksgivings together, attended our kids' soccer games together. His kids and mine were friends, and his wife and my wife were friends. In a sense, I was his superior, but I understood we were peers, and I wanted him to know that. I didn't want to flatter him or thank him; I just wanted him to know I knew. What I ended up saying was, "I think you're really going to miss me."

"I think I am," he said.

"I was joking," I said.

"I know," he said.

We rented a small U-Haul for the stuff we didn't want the movers to touch, the fragile and more-valuable objects. I remember I had to drive down to Florence a few days early because the house was still in escrow and I had to be there to sign a few documents and to report for duty.

Courtney stayed up in Ilwaco with the kids, running final errands and saying last-minute good-byes.

The truck we rented was one with two rear tires on each side, big and clumsy and hard to drive. When I got ninety minutes south of the Cape, I was near Tillamook and the truck started driving weirdly, pulling to the right. It was at a part of the highway, 101, where there were no pull-offs or exits or parking lots, just road, then cliff, then ocean, with no real barrier. There was nowhere to stop, nowhere to pull over, and the truck kept pulling right, toward the edge of the cliff. There was only a small, two-foot guardrail between me and two hundred feet of cliff and I could see straight down to where the waves crashed against the boulders. As I came around a bend, I lost control of the truck. I heard a loud bang, like a shotgun, and the truck lurched to the right and hit the guardrail. I felt the left-side wheels lift off the ground then come back down again. I had no brakes, no steering, no nothing, so I held on as the truck came to a rolling stop in the middle of the road. I put it into park, pulled the emergency brake, and got out.

The southbound traffic came whipping by me in the left lane, careening around the corners, honking their horns as I inspected the truck. The two passenger-side rear tires had come completely off, shredded into nothing somewhere back up the road. I could see the trail of black rubber shreds leading around the bend. The people at U-Haul were very apologetic and said they would give me a complete refund. They'd call a tow truck to come and tow me down to Florence. I waited on the side of the road for nearly an hour before the tow truck arrived, sitting on the guardrail where the truck had dented it. It gave me plenty of time to catch my breath and consider that below the flimsy guardrail it was just straight granite cliff and boulders and violent waters. There was no vegetation or brush to slow our fall.

The tow truck driver hooked the truck up to a hook and cable, and with the winch, lifted the rear wheels off the ground and onto his flatbed. It took about five more hours before we got to the house in Florence because we couldn't drive more than thirty miles per hour the whole way. The cab of the truck smelled of burnt oil. There was a can of Copenhagen in the center console. I asked the driver for a chew and he gave me the can and a plastic cup to spit in. I rolled up a wad of tobacco between my finger and thumb and placed it in the divot of my bottom lip. Out the passenger window I watched the ocean roll toward the horizon, spreading out, promising a new life, a new start, a terrifying new era.

Florence, Oregon, was our home for four years, a small fishing and logging town like so many others that dot the coastline. It was here that I coached Little League baseball and went to swim meets and softball games and volunteered at my kids' elementary school, and even went to an occasional PTA meeting. It was where I became a better father, navigating a steep learning curve.

I remember once Courtney left on a trip to Boston with her friend Tasha, who worked for the Coast Guard at Station Cape Disappointment. It was the first time Courtney had been away from any of the kids for longer than a couple of days. During that time I took on many of the household duties that typically fell to her, including getting the kids up for school, feeding them breakfast, making their lunches, picking them up from school, entertaining them for several hours, cooking dinner, bathing them, brushing their teeth, putting them to bed, and then waking them up the next morning and doing it all over again. It was a shock to my system. By Friday, I was so exhausted that I called in sick to work and let the kids sleep in. They missed school. At around nine a.m., the kids woke up and I drove them into town to rent some movies and brought them back home. Three hours later I got a call from Courtney.

"Are you kidding me?" she said. She told me she'd gotten a call from someone at the school, saying the kids hadn't shown up.

"I'm sorry, I was really tired," I said. "I couldn't get up this morning."

"I can't believe you," she said. "You're sorry. You were too tired?"

I tried to calm her, my voice pleading. I told her I was sorry again, but it was fine, I promised, really. The kids and I were safe and we were all at home just sitting in front of the TV, watching a movie.

"All right," she said. "But I'm still mad." I heard her voice go from frantic to panicked to calm within seconds. "I still can't believe you. I really was scared shitless, you know? You need to tell me if you're going to do that again."

"Okay," I said.

"You're such a jackass," she said, but I could tell she was smiling when she said it.

She hung up the phone.

Florence was also where the fifth and final member of our family was born. Our daughter Mia was born at the Peace Harbor Hospital in Florence on October 31, 2006, during a rivalry game between the Pittsburgh Steelers and the Baltimore Ravens. I only remember this now because the doctor kept giving us updates on the score. He was an Eagles fan. Looking back, Mia signified a change in our lives. For me, it was the beginning of the transition into being domesticated. That meant no more cases, no more boats or big waves, no more dead bodies. But it also meant a job inside an office. This is all just to say that the transition presented its own set of difficulties: I was taking a step back from a job I had invested a good deal of myself in, and was treading in unknown territory.

There was one time when I was watching Mia at the house and I lost her in a span of thirty minutes. She was two or three years old, and the older kids, Matthew and Taylor, were at school. Courtney was out running errands. I turned my head away for a second and she was gone, just gone. I ran around the house, looking through all the rooms, all the closets, screaming, pulling my hair out. I felt the heat rise to the surface of my skin, my heart racing. I looked for her everywhere, flipping over the cushions on the couch, turning over the mattresses, throwing clothes out of the closets, tearing through the garage and emptying the kitchen cabinets. She was nowhere. I was going to be sick. Something bitter and sour rose up in the back of my throat. I called Courtney.

"You what?" she said.

"I don't know. I can't find her," I said.

"How do you lose a baby?"

"I don't know. It wasn't my fault," I pleaded. "I turned away for just a second and she was gone."

"Jesus Christ, Christopher. Where did you last see her?"

"We were in the living room," I said.

"All right," she said. "I'm coming home."

Everything turned out to be okay. By the time Courtney got home, I had found Mia sleeping beneath one of the bunkbeds with a blanket wrapped around her. It took me an hour, and I remember thinking for every excruciating moment of that hour that I simply wasn't cut out for this. Even though she was safe I would suffer the wrath of her worried mother.

Another time, I remember Mia got a small blue bead stuck up her nose while under my watch. The bead was not just inside her nostril; it was really stuck. Where she'd gotten the bead from was anyone's guess, and when I tried to get it out it, I probably pushed it further up. Mia was crying and screaming. I called Courtney on the way to the emergency room. These kinds of calls were always the most difficult to make. I felt infinitely small when I had to tell Courtney I'd messed up. I had to admit I wasn't paying attention when Mia shoved it up her nose so far it was lodged up in her septum, where it bulged beneath her eye. The doctor didn't know how to get it out but gave her a lollipop coated with pain-killers, which calmed her down. To make a long story short, after an hour of debate about how to proceed, the doctor used a long wooden stick to pop the bead out of her nose, as if he were shucking a mussel off a rock. The tiny blue bead that had caused us all so much pain came shooting out, like a tiny comet covered in blood and snot.

Before I left for Station Siuslaw, I was promoted to chief. I studied for the exam, a fifty-question test covering basic military protocol, administration, budget management, law enforcement protocol, armory management, rate and rank, and basic navigation. It was the second time I'd taken the test. I had taken it a few years before and scored in the top fifty, but because I didn't have enough under-way time and hands-on experience, I didn't score enough points to make rank. This time around I did worse on the written exam, but because I had amassed so much under-way time on the Columbia, I was promoted to the rank of chief—second-in-command at the station.

My first week at Station Siuslaw a boy drowned at the mouth of the river. It was an enigma. No one at the station could remember anything like this happening within the past five years. While such drownings weren't unheard of, they simply didn't happen very often, maybe once or twice every ten years. The conditions on the Siuslaw River were mild compared to those on the Columbia, making it a rare event. The bar at the Siuslaw was not nearly as big, and it was not a good spot for salmon fishing, so it drew fewer boats. The salmon simply never ran up the Siuslaw like they did up the Columbia. Over my three-year tour at Station Siuslaw I personally ran only five or six more cases after this one, none of them involving drowning or death, and none of them involved a child. I felt cursed. The memory of the Russian girl and her red shoes was still fresh in my mind, and I felt like I couldn't escape whatever I imagined was chasing me.

Recently when I was talking to Kyle Hoag we were reminiscing about old cases, and I told him about the Russian girl case. He laughed, not out of malice or ill will, but because he'd had something similar happen to him. He told me about a case he'd run about six years before in which he'd had to pull a boy out of the water off the coast of Southern California, near the Channel Islands. The boy, he said, was wearing similar Converse high-tops when they picked him up. It was the shoes that broke him, that forced him into retirement and eventually to finding a civilian job with NOAA in Alaska. Now, he said, he can't look at a pair of Converse sneakers without shuddering. I knew what he meant.

Those of us drawn to the ocean are susceptible to such superstitions. We seek out answers to death's mysteries in signs of fate, omens, sometimes curses. For a while, I blamed myself for the unusual drowning of the boy who died when I first arrived at Siuslaw, convinced I had brought some nasty wind from the waters up north.

I remember BM2 Ross Meyers was driving that day, but he was driving tentatively. We were right along the shore, next to the beach, and I could see the wind whipping wisps of sand off the sand dunes. The water was a murky brown color, almost reddish. There was a thick fog bank rolling in, so the visibility was not very good, and declining rapidly. There was a volunteer beach command walking the beach, searching the coastline, calling out crab pot buoys over the radio. For ten minutes, we drove around in circles.

"Do you mind if I drive?" I asked Meyers.

"You sure?" he said.

"Yeah."

I took the boat closer to the beach. As long as you know where the shoals and reefs are, a beach is a beach. I got within a hundred yards, to where the Fathometer couldn't get a reading and we started churning up sand, and I knew we couldn't get any closer. I drove the boat north, turned around, and drove back south. Then, someone in the volunteer beach command spotted him.

It was just his head sticking out of the water, but he was facedown. His head looked like a crab pot buoy. We got within twenty yards of him when he sank, quickly and without warning. He just sank. I had heard of bodies doing this but I'd never seen it happen. When someone drowns, built-up gas in the body brings it to the surface, but after a couple hours the gas dissipates and the body sinks again, where it usually remains for good. I'm not sure if the body of the boy ever washed up again. If so, I never heard about it.

We heard the boy had Crohn's disease and supposedly had gone swimming off the North Jetty when his muscles seized and he drowned. He was on summer vacation with his family, including his mother, father, younger sister, and grandparents. I suffered through bouts of superstition afterward: For weeks I couldn't help imagining that this boy had died for a reason, and that I was part of that reason—that somehow this boy had drowned in place of the Russian girl's brother. Somehow his death was my punishment. I was cursed, and I had brought the curse down here from the waters off the Cape and unleashed it.

Time proved that none of this was true, of course. There was no curse, no cosmic conspiracy of any kind. There was no force of evil, no demons or ghosts following in my wake. After this initial, humbling fatality I skated through the next several years at Siuslaw untouched by death. I didn't see another dead body for nearly another decade. I worked my way up the chain of command, becoming ever more entrenched in the bureaucracy of the US military. Then without the smallest warning I was felled by an unforeseen health problem and subsequently medically discharged from the Coast Guard.

I currently live in Slidell, Louisiana, with my wife and children. At the time of my retirement, I held the rank of CWO3 of Station New Orleans, tasked with overseeing a division of law and drug enforcement. I sat at a desk all day. I pushed pencils and filed paperwork. Our priority at the station was boat boardings, drug interdiction, security patrols, and search and rescue on the Gulf of Mexico. It was a far cry from the search-and-rescue cases I ran on the waters off the Oregon and Washington coasts.

When the Coast Guard decided they needed me in New Orleans more than they needed me at Siuslaw, we put the green house on the market and prepared for a major move. The timing was bad: The recession of 2007–2008 was deep, and there were millions of homes for sale everywhere across the country. Why would anyone move to coastal Oregon, a spot popular with retirees but not exactly flush with jobs? We found out the hard way that they wouldn't, and the house sat on the market. It was nearly impossible to raise three kids and keep current on mortgage payments while living at our new station in Louisiana. Our savings were draining away as our anxiety ratcheted up.

Everywhere, Coast Guard personnel like us were sinking into debt over homes we were obligated to pay for but could not sell, and yet we couldn't live in them because we were transferred on a regular basis. Worse, the situation could destroy us professionally, because if a Coast Guardsman walks away from a home or other financial obligation that they cannot afford, it reflects on our ability to do our jobs. We can be denied a security clearance for financial misdeeds, and potentially lose our jobs. I was worried for myself and for my colleagues.

Just before we left for New York to watch my son Matthew play in the Little League World Series at Cooperstown, my contact at our mortgage company promised she had a buyer for us. We were on cloud nine for a while, sure that the worst was over. Yet in the middle of the series, while I was rooting for Matthew's team and trying not to be distracted by the real estate transaction, the same person called again to say the sale had fallen through.

When I got that message I almost lost my footing. Her words echoed in my head. I had to sit down to absorb the blow. I wanted to throw up—to cry. The news was as bad as any wave I'd ever taken, yet the waves would always subside eventually. I'd come out the other side with the foam receding from the boat and turn back to the station, dry out, and recover. This financial blow was worse because the hole just kept getting deeper, and I couldn't find the bottom to start trying to climb out. Every direction in which I tried to navigate seemed hopeless. We'd even borrowed from my parents, a situation no adult with a career and a family ever wants to get into. It was humiliating.

A day later the situation reversed: The mortgage company approved the buyer. I didn't know what my contact had done to make that deal happen, but I will forever be grateful. We were free of the house and the black cloud of potential career repercussions, albeit scarred and broken financially. As far as I know there was no official memo or policy change about letting Coast Guardsmen keep their security clearances even if they walked away from a house in foreclosure during that period, but the brass seemed to look the other way. I never heard of anyone getting discharged or losing their clearance as a result of the recession. I guess the financial damage was enough punishment; it was more than enough for me.

After a while in Slidell I missed the Pacific Ocean, the rain and the cold and the waves, and watching the weather turn into a gale force of wind and rain and waves so ferocious it was as if only some higher being could conjure such magnificence. I missed the changes in seasons. I missed being out on the water, on a boat. I tell Courtney this every now and then, just as a way of reminding her of my dissatisfaction with Louisiana.

"Then move back there," she jokes. "I don't care. But me and the kids are staying put right here."

After two years in New Orleans, I was offered a command position back in Oregon, in Grays Harbor or Newport or Umpqua. When I ran the idea by Courtney and the kids it was met with complete and total opposition. Both Matthew and Taylor were in high school by this point, and Mia was starting elementary school that year. Courtney had a job at a daycare and a community of close friends. It was a unanimous decision; none of them wanted to leave. I couldn't blame them. They were comfortable here, and I couldn't ask them to relocate again, just because I was unhappy. I turned down the position.

I knew how painful relocation was, especially for the kids; anyone who works for the military knows this. It is something I will never forget, the day we said good-bye to our home in Ilwaco and drove the four and a half hours south to Florence. I will never forget finding the kids hiding in the closet in their bedroom, refusing to leave and accusing us of wrongdoing, a couple hours before we closed the front door for the last time on the only home they'd known. The kids were inconsolable almost the whole way, crying and protesting, and nothing Courtney and I were saying was getting through to them—our promises and reassurances that everything would be okay. We drove south along I-101 in silence. No one spoke. After a while the kids calmed down some and fell asleep to the sound of the droning engine. Outside, the trees and the ocean and the clouds zoomed pitifully past our windows.

Summer turned to autumn and autumn to winter, and once again the days folded into darkness. The poplar and maple reddened and yellowed and shed their leaves and all along the quiet streets were raked into piles by the curb. The weeks of rain and endless gray came once again to the coast. Six months into my tour at Station Siuslaw, the master chief was put on leave for roughing up one of the crewmen. I was on leave myself, visiting family and friends in California for the holidays. I got a phone call from the group commander out of North Bend while at my parents' house. He told me the master chief had grabbed one of the crewmen by the shoulders and shaken him and thrown him against a wall.

"Jesus," I said.

"Yeah," he said. "Another crewman reported that he even tried to strangle the other guy, but others say that didn't happen. I don't know."

"Jesus," I said again.

"What's your opinion of him?"

I wasn't surprised, was what I wanted to say.

"The master chief?" I said. "Well, I don't know."

"Okay," he said. "I get it. It's a lot. You're on vacation. Do you think you can report to my office when you get back?"

I rogered.

When I got back to Florence, I reported to his office in Coos Bay. My work on the Columbia River had gained me some notoriety and respect from some of the higher-ups. I told him I thought the master chief was shady, a bit paranoid. I told him he micromanaged the crew and led by intimidation, which was all true. The term I used was "rock management." He ordered his crew to get a rock, and when they came back with a rock, he told them to get a different rock, and so on and so on. I didn't think it was an efficient use of resources. He got the idea. I left. Five days later, the group commander came into my office at Station Siuslaw and put me in charge of the station.

"At least until we find a replacement for him," he said.

"What happened to him?"

"He was reappointed."

Before I could argue or ask questions, he left. On paper, I was in charge of the station for around a year. I was not promoted to master chief. I kept my same rate and rank, but I was the officer in charge. I was in command. No more master chief. Everyone at the station seemed pretty relieved—everyone except me. Even though the previous master chief was a bully and kind of an arrogant meathead, he did take care of a lot of the daily routines. There was still a station to run, an entire crew to manage, all without an official chief or commander. I was it. I was all they had.

One of my jobs was to oversee the training of the next generation of search-and-rescuers, break-in coxswains and surfmen. And because we only ran half the number of cases, it left us with a lot of spare time to do surf training.

One day that winter, a big storm from up north came in and the swell was so big that most of the bars up and down the coast had to shut down to commercial traffic. I wanted to take some of the crew out there to see what it was like to be in some heavy surf. Umpqua and Newport were all over twenty feet, while the Siuslaw Bar was pushing maybe fifteen. Once I heard that the Columbia had been closed, I waited for an hour or so to see if ours would be closed.

It never happened.

At the time, it was my call. The captain of the port wasn't going to close the Bar, so I decided we should do some surf training. I hadn't been on a boat in heavy weather like this in a few months, and there weren't many opportunities to train in weather like this, so I jumped at any and every chance that came up. We did beach training, which is a little different than bar training. On the Bar, if something bad happened, you either got sucked out to the ocean or pushed back into the river; but if something happened while close to the beach, if the boat rolled or capsized, your boat would hit bottom or would get pushed up onto the shore.

We were making an inbound run near the north side of the jetty. About ten minutes passed and we took several big breaks, running the boat over and through the waves. I could tell some of the boat crewmen were getting kind of rattled out there. They were clipped in to their surf belts, but I knew some of them hadn't ever been in surf this terrifying before. It looked like the swell was picking up too, getting bigger with the incoming tide. We had been out on the water for not even a half-hour before I called it. It was simply too big for any kind of real training. I knew we would just end up getting stuck out here.

I radioed the other lifeboat and told them we were going to lateral out.

I checked the Fathometer and it was reading about thirty-four feet of depth. I wasn't worried because typically waves don't break in thirty feet of water. But as we were preparing to exit the surf zone, the other lifeboat called in and said there was another big set coming in. If I had to guess, I would say the waves were pushing twenty-five feet, breaking top to bottom. When the set approached, I could see the tops of the waves feathering. I knew it wasn't good, immediately. I knew we would either be pinned to the bottom or the wave would push us onto the beach. We were in the worst possible spot.

I told the crew to hang on. The third wave was going to break on us, though I didn't tell them this. Once it was a hundred yards in front of us, I pushed down on the throttles, going about as fast as the boat could go.

When the wave broke, it broke right on top of us. It felt like doing a full sprint and running straight into a concrete wall. The boat rattled and shook, as the force of the wave pushed us downward into sand. Then there was this brief moment of weightlessness as we went under the wave. Everything was absolutely silenced, all noises drowned out, until we pushed through the back.

As soon as we came to the surface, all hell broke loose. Every alarm on the boat was going off. There was flooding in the engine room. The crew looked at each other, from face to face, then started to check themselves for injuries. Everyone seemed to be okay, but the looks on their faces were unforgettable. It was the same one on mine, I was sure. We were all terrified, scared shitless.

I started to assess the damage. The enclosed bridge was crushed, flattened beyond repair. Three windows, which were an inch and a half thick, were shattered and blown out, and most of the electronics belowdecks were haywiring.

When we got back to the station and were tying up the boat, the engineer came up to me.

"Chief," he said. "You okay?"

"Yeah," I said. "I think so."

"That might be the first time I have ever seen you scared."

"That's probably not true," I said.

"I mean, that's the first time I've seen that look on your face. Concerned, I guess I'd call it."

I wasn't shaking or trembling, but I was scared. My heart was still racing. I could feel it caught in the back of my throat.

Then I said, "We really had no business being out there."

When I got home, I told Courtney I might lose my job. I was scared. I had done hundreds of thousands of dollars' worth of damage to a boat, not to mention putting the lives and the well-being of four of my coworkers at risk.

The captain from the Office of Boat Forces called me at my office the following day. I think it was the captain. His job was to ensure that those in command or in positions of authority were not abusing their power or misusing their resources. He went in front of a board of officers and told them I should essentially be fired. I didn't dispute it. He drew diagrams and brought up spreadsheets, showing that all the other bars along the coast had been closed. Someone in Washington supposedly wanted my head on a platter.

Courtney told me it would be okay.

"How do you know?" I said. "I can get in pretty big trouble here."

"I don't know. I just do. It'll work out."

She was two months pregnant with Mia at the time, just beginning to show. Though I wasn't entirely convinced by what she'd said, her words comforted me.

I didn't yet know that my group commander would come to my rescue. He called me a couple days later from his office in North Bend.

"I don't want you to worry," he said. "You were doing exactly what you were supposed to be doing. You were training these kids to drive boats in the serious shit. That's your job."

He told me he'd gone in front of another board of officers to defend my case, saying, "Things like this are just a part of the business." He'd told them I was just doing my job—that he had the utmost confidence in me to carry out my duties in a professional and responsible manner. He reminded them of some of my achievements and awards, and asked the board to show a little lenience.

I winced when I heard he'd said that, even though I knew he was just trying to protect me. In the end, it worked. I was let off with nothing more than a slap on the wrist.

Everything seemed to change after that. To make things even better, my assignment officer in DC found a replacement master chief a few weeks later, and I was no longer in command at the station. I'm not sure what I felt when I heard the news. Relief, I guess. I was tried, and tired. I needed a break. Courtney was in her second trimester, growing larger and larger with each day, more beautiful. At night, she fell asleep in the rocker in the baby's room, where I sometimes found her when I got home from work, rubbing her stomach, half-smiling.

When I told her the news, she smiled and reached out and grabbed my hand.

"I told you things would work out," she said.

Later that night, we ate dinner. Spaghetti and meatballs.

Once we'd moved to Florence, eating dinner together every night became part of our routine, something predictable for the kids to rely on. For me, too. No more late nights spent on duty, eating in the mess hall at the station or sleeping on the couch in the rec lounge. Growing up now meant focusing on family and spending quality time with them. Not allowing the work to consume me. Not allowing myself to dwell on the things I couldn't change, all the death and violence the waters of the Columbia had brought into my life.

I had lived off it for almost seven years, like a junkie. I'd let it creep into my skin, like a slack rain. But there was a tension, still. Because I felt like I needed to be around more to become a better father and husband, it meant there was less room for caring about the work. Eventually, I just stopped. The death of the boy a few months earlier and the death of the girl a few months before that weren't the least bit on my mind. Not anymore. They were gone. I was present. Here, eating dinner with my family.

Matthew had spaghetti sauce smeared on his face. Taylor was at the stage in her life when silence was her default. It was raining, as it always was. I stared out the window, watching the rain streak down the panes.

After dinner, Courtney tucked the kids into bed and read them a bedtime story. I cleared the table and put the dishes in the sink. Then I stepped outside to sit beside the river in the streaming red light of dusk. I sat and watched the pools of murky water swirl in the shallows, where the last of the year's mosquitoes had laid their eggs. The coast was drenched in fog and rain and streaks of colored sky peeked through the gray fog banks. The last of the sunlight on the hills flashed red then orange then gold, further west, to where the ocean that holds nothing back becomes a tomb for ships and lost travelers. A heavy wind halted the incoming boats. A light rain blew downriver and out to sea and was gone.

Epilogue

One minute I was sitting on the couch talking to Courtney while she made dinner and the next I was waking up in the hospital with a nurse asking me questions I was too groggy to answer. That was more than five years ago, while stationed at Base New Orleans.

In the hospital I didn't know where I was or how I'd gotten there. I was confused, disoriented, and nauseous. The nurse kept asking me questions, but I was just trying to figure out how I'd gone from my couch to being hooked up to machines, with tubes in my arm. I'd never had a blackout before, at least none that I knew of—none that had sidelined me or caused me to lose consciousness.

They told me I had extremely low blood pressure and that my heart rate was exceedingly low. The doctor said he didn't know what was wrong with me before referring me to specialists.

Over the next few months, I saw several neurologists and a couple of cardiologists, but none of them could tell me what it was. They couldn't tell me if it was hereditary or genetic, how serious it was, or how much longer I would continue to live. Finally, I got a diagnosis from a cardiologist, who recommended I get surgery at the Mayo Clinic in Rochester, Minnesota. He told me that I have a vascular disorder. For whatever reason, my heart grew tilted and bent on an axis, with three valves rather than four, and my veins siphon deoxygenated blood from my brain to my heart. The doctor couldn't explain why.

"God must have been smoking a huge joint when he made you," he joked. When I asked him how serious it was, he didn't joke. He said it's very serious.

Cape Disappointment is now fifteen years in the past, and it's been more than a decade since I've been on a boat in the surf. Even if I wanted to go back, I wouldn't be able to. The episodes are unpredictable. I get bad headaches and nausea and my hands turn blue if I exert myself too much.

I no longer work in the field of search and rescue. For a while I was commanding officer for Station New Orleans, doing law enforcement, filing paperwork and sending it down the proper channels of bureaucracy. Now I take care of chores around the house, keeping it clean, and I take our youngest daughter Mia to school in the morning, make her lunch, and take her to swim practice in the afternoon. Courtney manages the child-care center at the local gym. Taylor and Matthew are old enough to drive. Matthew works a job at the same gym where Courtney works, which she helped him get. Our children are older now but they are still growing up, still learning; they need Courtney and me less and less each year, which is a good thing, and something she told me we should be proud of.

I know I might not get to experience the rest of what is considered a long and happy life. I know I might not get to see my children grow into fully formed, responsible adults. I might not get to watch them find their passions, their callings, or find companionship and love. I might not be there when they stumble and fall and get back up, then learn from their mistakes. As much as I'd like to, I may not be there if one day they get married and have kids of their own. It's possible that none of this is in the stars for me.

But I also know I was lucky enough to have made my mark, to have had the love and support of my family, and to have done the work I love. I want my children to know that, and I want the same for them. I want them to know me not just as the guy who does their laundry and cleans their dishes and brings them to school and takes Nitrostat on a regular basis. I want them to know who I was.

Acknowledgments

THIS BOOK IS FIRST AND FOREMOST DEDICATED TO MY WIFE, COURTNEY, my daughters, Taylor and Mia, and my son, Matthew. Anyone who has ever been a spouse or a child of a service member will tell you how difficult the life is, especially the first few years. My family was no different. Without all their support and love, I know full well my career would not have been the same.

So, to my loving, caring, and supportive wife, my deepest gratitude. Your encouragement when times were rough is more than appreciated. Just knowing you would be there when I had a hard day at work made a difficult and sometimes terrifying job much more bearable. It was a relief knowing you were keeping our household and kids happy and safe while I was working. I know I will never be able to thank you enough. You bring joy and inspiration to my life. I love you.

To Taylor, Matthew, and Mia, you have always been my motivation, my source of inspiration to aim higher, to set a good example, to be the best person I can be. That is what I have always hoped to achieve: to make you proud. You were all probably too young to remember what my career entailed, so this book is in many ways for you. I hope you will read it one day and hopefully understand me in a new light. I love you.

Judy and John D'Amelio, Mom and Dad, I want to thank you from the bottom of my heart for always supporting me and being there for me. I am a much better person because of you. From childhood to adulthood you have been the difference makers. No matter what the circumstances, I know I can always count on you for advice or a friendly ear. I truly believe I would not be where I am or who I am today if it wasn't for you. I love you.

Gene and Marsha Wada, I couldn't have asked for greater or more-involved in-laws. You have always been there, not only for me, but for our entire family. From our exhausting road trips to being there for the kids while we were away, I more than appreciate everything you have done for our family. Thank you.

Reid Maruyama, this book never would have happened without your hard work, belief, and dedication. Knowing little about the Coast Guard, you quickly absorbed what most people would have taken years to learn. From the time you spent at Station Cape Disappointment to the countless hours of interviews to the research and books you read, you are the one who made this all happen. I can't stress this enough. If it wasn't for you, this entire project would have never come together. I can't thank you enough.

Allison O'Leary, I want to thank you for all the hard work you put into this project and all the advice you have given me. Your support, encouragement, and knowledge helped to make this book possible. Thank you.

I also want to thank the following people for helping me with this book and for making my tour at Cape Disappointment a memorable one. To my friends and extended family, I would like to extend my love and gratitude: Dave and Brooke Hofkins, Kevin Rhodes, Casey Verdugo, and Kyle Knudson. To my family in the Coast Guard, my life in the Pacific Northwest wouldn't have been the same without you: Scott and Beth Slade, Tyler and Shan Bartel, Tom Karczewski, Joel Abstetar, Jamie Frederick, Tisha Aurechio, Jeff Kihlmire, Jason Linnett, Jamie Frederick, Wes Parker, Michael Hoag, Ralph Gilbert, Jeff Kotson, Michael Loizakes, Dr. William Jeffrey Long, Dan Johnson, and Fred Bowman. And finally, to Dr. Dennis Noble, David Hofkins, and Michael Tougias—thank you for encouraging me to write this book.

There have been countless people in the Coast Guard who have helped to train and mentor me throughout my career. I know I haven't mentioned everyone by name, so to all of those I failed to mention,

I just want to thank you for all the knowledge and leadership you provided me and the communities we served. To the Crew of Station Cape Disappointment (1997–2005), the Crew of Station Siuslaw River (2005–2008), and the Crew of Station Umpqua River (2008–2009), I thank you.

Index

Photo plates are indicated by "p": p1, p2, p3, etc.

accidents: at Cape D, 42–44; decapitation accident, 51–53; truck accident, 173–74. *See also* helicopter accidents

achievement medals, 149

Adkins, Kaleb, 64–66, 69–72, 126–27; at Camp Rilea helicopter crash, 81–83; as friend and peer, 172; as surfman, 86–87

Admiral Benson (steam ship), 77

admiration, 73

adoption, 24

adrenaline surges, 44, 61, 95, 122, 140

AFRAS. *See* Association for Rescue at Sea

A Jetty, Columbia River, 4, 61, 121; shipwreck at, 77; surfing at, 44–46, 85–87; view of, 40; waves at, 125

Alameda, California, 17, 26, 27

Alaska: crab fleet, 17, 163; Hoag in, 177; Kodiak, 18, 21–22, 31; three-month-long trips to, 17, 22, 29–31; weather in, 116, 147, 153

Aleuts, 19

anxiety, 13, 179

aptitude, x

Aptos, California: childhood in, ix, 22–23, 41; as hometown, 83; leaves in, 42; surfing in, 41

Arctic Circle, 26

arrogance, 40, 41

Association for Rescue at Sea (AFRAS) awards, p2, p5, p6, 101; arrival at, 146–47; ceremony at White House, 147–49; Collins presenting, 150–54; D'Amelio, Courtney, attending, 146–47; for dedication, judgment, devotion to duty, 140; gold medal, 145–46, 148, 153; Kinsey receiving medal, 145–46; recipients of, 150–51; speech at, 153; summary of Peacock Spit rescue, 152–53; unease at, 148–50

Astoria-Megler Bridge, Columbia River, 114; searches at, 90, 118; suicides and, 88–90; as terrorist target, 113 awards: to Coast Guard Auxiliary, 150–51; committees for, 101; White House ceremony, 147–48. *See also* Association for Rescue at Sea awards; commendations; medals

Baker Bay channel, Columbia River, 61–63, 70, 87; breakers at, 66–67
Baltimore Ravens, 175
barbecues, 61, 64, 161, 172
bar pilots, 41, 96–97, 118–19
Baymist (fishing boat), 83–85
beach command, 134, 135, 136, 177, 178
Beast Coast (crab boat): as disabled boat, 114–17; fire and sinking of, 120; seizure of, 119
Benson Beach, Cape Disappointment State Park, 5, 61, 121; capsized boat at, 126
Beretta handguns, 112
Bering Sea, 17, 113; last trip, 30–31; search-and-rescue in, 26; St. Paul Island, 18–21; unpredictable weather of, 19
Bettie M (wreck), 45, 77
Big Sur, California, ix
blind spots, 97, 130
BM3. *See* boatswain's mate
boats: *Admiral Benson*, 77; boat boardings, 33, 114, 117, 118, 179; boat maneuvering, 42, 130–31, 135–37, 152; boat pilots, 41, 79, 96; boat

seizures, 119; broken-down, 166; *Chinook*, 96–97; *Isabella*, 77; maintenance of USCG, 85; National Motor Lifeboat School, 40–41, 44, 47; Office of Boat Forces, 184; over boat limitations, 64–65; USS *Peacock*, 77; *Peter Iredale*, 77; pleasure crafts, 3, 128; Recreational Boating Safety Patrol, 3; rule against leaving, 8; small boat stations, vii–viii; Triumph motor lifeboat, 42, 51, 99, 162; weather and, 42. *See also* capsized boats; cargo freighters; disabled boats; fishing boats; *Long Island*; *Sherman*; shipwrecks; tows and escorts
boatswain's mate (BM3), 33, 121
bombs, 90, 113, 118
bomb searches, 90, 112–13
boot camp, USCG, 24–26
Boston, 149, 174
bravery, 44, 101, 128
breakers, 159; at Baker Bay channel, 66–67; boat-busting, 4; eighteen-foot, 96; at North Jetty, 130; at Peacock Spit, 137, 152; twenty-foot, 63. *See also* weather
Brewer, Bill, 51–52
Buoy 10 Fishery, Columbia River, 4, 43, 61, 77, 96, 126
bureaucrats, 18–19
Burkes, Dan, 47
burn victim rescue, 77–79

Cabrillo College, Aptos, California, 23

Camp Rilea, Oregon, 81–83

Canada, 26

Cape Disappointment (Cape D), Ilwaco, Washington, vii; accidents at, 42–44; burn victim rescue, 77–79; changing directives at, 117–18; close calls at, 42; constantly changing weather at, 117, 159; decapitation accident, 51–53; extreme weather at, 51, 63; farewell party, 171–72; first arrival at, 39; first big case, 61–63; gates and barricades at, 112; gym at, 95; as home, 83; home life at, 61; landscape of, 35; Mother Nature and, 117; rain at, 51; responsibilities at, 85; risk-taking reputation at, 54; Russian child drowning at, 3–13, 161, 164–65, 177; search-and-rescue at, 5, 34; security patrols at, 161; summer as busy season, 3; *that guy* at, 5; tows and escorts at, 61–73; transfer from, 13, 161; transfer to, 34

Cape May, New Jersey, 24–26

Capitola Junior Lifeguards, 24

capsized boats, 6, 13, 21, 86–87; at Benson Beach, 126; at Clatsop Spit, 145–46; at Peacock Spit, 121–22, 128–40; survivors, 122, 138, 152; training boat as, 43–44

Captain, notorious fisherman: condescension and criticism from, 117; first meeting, 113–15; obscenities from, 119; unlawful fishing by, 116, 120

cargo freighters, 117–19; *Tampa*, 151

Chandler, Henry ("Cleve"), 150–51

Channel Islands, California, 177

Chatterman, Don, 119

chewing tobacco, 127, 174

chief rank, 176

childhood, 24; in Aptos, California, ix, 22–23; on ocean, 53; surfing, 44

children: fears of new father, 32; fist born, 34; inward looking on, 188; joy in, 34; planning for, 29–30; second born, 61; third born, 175. *See also* fatherhood

Chinook (pilot boat), 96–97

Christmas vacation, 2001, 120

CISM. *See* Critical Incident Stress Management

Clatsop Spit, Columbia River, 39, 54, 56, 77; capsized boat at, 145–46; disabled boats at, 95–101; formation of, 145

Coast Guard Auxiliary, 83–85, 125; awards to, 150–51; medals to, 150

Cole's Barbecue, Aptos, California, 22

Collins, Thomas, p5; Department of Homeland Security and, 149; presenting AFRAS awards, 150–54

Colombia, 26
Columbia River Bar, 3–4, 6, 61;
    extreme weather at, 67–70;
    as Graveyard of the Pacific,
    5, 51, 77, 91; Halibut Derby,
    161, 165; notoriety from, 182;
    scale of, 67; shipwrecks in, 77,
    80–81; temperamental weather
    at, 39–40; tragic history of,
    77–80; watchtower cliff,
    39–40
commendations, viii, 153;
    achievement medals, 149; for
    acts of courage, 128; from
    peers and general public, 140.
    See also medals
Comms watch, 4–5; in Puzzle
    Palace, 125; reporting to, 7–9,
    39, 62, 88, 95, 132–33; support
    from, 99; training for, 83. *See
    also* watchstanders
communications skills, 41
constant moves, viii, 181
courage, 23, 25, 150;
    commendations for, 128
coxswain rank, 41, 51, 61, 105
CPR, 133–34
crab fishermen, 116
Critical Incident Stress
    Management (CISM), 83
Crohn's disease, 178
cruelty, 52, 83
curses, 51, 177–78

D'Amelio, Chris, p1, p2, p3, p5, 8.
    See also specific topics

D'Amelio, Courtney (wife), p1, 12,
    20, 42, 45, 146; arrival at Cape
    D, 39; at awards ceremony,
    146–47; Boston trip of, 174–
    75; Christmas vacation and,
    120; with family, 160, 188; first
    house of, 171; first meeting
    and dating, 22–23; marriage to,
    22, 27–28, 83; phone calls to,
    25–26; planning for children,
    29–30; pregnancy of, 31–32;
    reassurance from, 101, 141,
    147–49, 185; reprimands from,
    21–22, 32, 174–75; routine of,
    53; separations from, 27–29,
    148; at suicide site, 89–90;
    therapy of, 30
D'Amelio, Joey (uncle), 148–49
D'Amelio, John (father), 23–24, 27,
    111, 148–49
D'Amelio, Judy (mother), 24
D'Amelio, Matthew (son), p1, 12,
    64, 90, 188; at beach, 154;
    birth of, 61, 159; cradling of,
    160–61; fishing with, 154–55;
    at Little League World Series,
    179; relocation and, 181
D'Amelio, Mia (daughter), p1, p4,
    188; birth of, 175; losing track
    of, 175–76; stuck bead and,
    176
D'Amelio, Taylor (daughter), p1, 12,
    42, 45, 64, 188; at beach, 154;
    birth of, 34, 53; fishing with,
    154–55; independence of, 159;
    relocation and, 181

Damico, Alan, 131–32, 153–54; medal to, 153–54

Davenport, California, 44

death: certainty of, 46; confronting, 101; dealing with, viii, 88–89; fear of, 45; life-or-death situations, 6; mysteries of, 177; stress management and, 83. *See also* drownings; Russian child drowning; suicides

decapitation accident, 51–53

dedication, 83, 85, 114, 153

Department of Fish and Wildlife, 119

devotion to duty, 153

disabled boats, 17; *Beast Coast*, 114–17; at Clatsop Spit, 95–101; fireworks and, 165–67; fishing from, 162–65; *Linnea*, 96–101; *Pacific Sun*, 65–71; as routine, 63. *See also* tows and escorts

drownings, 86–87, 145; body recovery, 126–27; care of body, 105–6; case of Hoag, 177; dreams of, 155; of fishermen, 51, 81; helmets for victims, 106–8; at Peacock Spit, 106–7; in Peacock Spit high-profile capsized boat case, 132–39; at Siuslaw Station, 176–78. *See also* Russian child drowning; suicides

drug smugglers, 27, 32–33; counter-drug enforcement, 149; drug interdiction at New Orleans Station, 179

drunkenness, 31, 115, 147, 166

East Sand Island, Columbia River, 77, 87–89

Ecuador, 26

Eliot, Josh, 138–39

El Niño, 35

EMS, 70, 134, 135, 138

EMT classes, 23

equator, 26

Executive Officer (XO), 41, 100

exhaustion, 71

expectations, viii, 30, 80

Farr, Sam, p2, 140, 149

fate, 46, 177

fatherhood, 17, 83; changes for, 53; decision-making in, 164; demands of, 61; early months of, 148; fear of, 30, 32; learning curve for, 174; planning for, 29–31; worries of, 159

fear: after 9/11 terrorist attacks, 112; of death, 45; of failure, 48; of fatherhood, 30, 32; Russian child drowning and, 165; in SAR, 66; stories of, vii, 80; weakness and, 164

fireman, 128

fireworks, 165–67

fishermen, 77, 119, 146, 154; crab fishermen, 116; Department of Fish and Wildlife, 119; drowning of, 51, 81; drunken, 166; equipment of, 161; fishing from disabled boat, 162–65; keeping watch on, 3–4; quotas for, 64, 163; retired, 83–84. *See also* Captain, notorious

fisherman; fishing boats;
Peacock Spit, high-profile
capsized boat case
fishing boats, 126; Alaska crab
fleet, 17; *Baymist*, 83–85; *Beast
Coast*, 114–17, 119–20; *Gypsy*,
77–79; *Linnea*, 96–101; *Pacific
Sun*, 65–71; salmon boats, 3–4,
119; *Sea King*, 80–81
foot injury, 19–21, 28
forgiveness, 139, 164
fuel sheen, 82

Giles, Jerry, 128, 134, 137
Gracey, James, 149
gratitude, 73
Graveyard of the Pacific, Cape
Disappointment, Washington,
5, 51, 77, 91
Grays Harbor, Oregon, 180
Green Bay Packers, 147
grief, 12–13
Group Astoria, 80, 82, 121; orders
from, 112–13; reports to,
131–34
guard duty, 112–13
guilt, 29, 63, 73; over Russian child
drowning, 11, 164–65; over
Siuslaw Station drowning, 177
Gulf of Mexico, 179
Gypsy (crab boat), 77–79

Half Moon Bay, California, 44
Halibut Derby, Columbia River,
161, 165
Hawaii, 26

Hayes, Steve, 95
helicopter accidents: Camp Rilea
crash, 81–83; foot injury from,
17–20
helicopter pilots, 9–11, 68–69,
121, 128, 137; lack of
understanding in, 134–35
helicopter tie-down crew, 17
helplessness, 9–10, 111, 148
heroism, 150; job in, 81; recognition
and language of, 140; stories
of, vii, 80, 128
Hoag, Kyle, 41, 47; advice from,
48; in Alaska, 177; drowning
case of, 177; reporting to, 121;
school of thought, 54; as XO,
41, 100
Hofkins, Dave, 27–28, 44
homeless people, 147
honor, 140, 150
Hudson Bay Company, 77

ice floes, 26
illegal fishing, 114, 116, 119–20
Ilwaco, Washington, 100. *See also*
Cape Disappointment, Ilwaco,
Washington
instincts, 11, 134, 164
integrity, 23, 25
International Date Line, 26
inward looking, x, 35, 188
Isabella (wreck), 77
isolated duty stations, 19

Jaws of Ilwaco, Washington, 100
judgment, 140, 153

Kennewick, Washington, 117
Kenyon, Charles, 44
King Neptune, 26
Kinsey, Sam, AFRAS medal to, 145–46
Klickitat, Washington, 117
Kodiak, Alaska, 18, 21–22, 31
Korean War Veterans Memorial, 147

Lake Michigan, 163
Lake Superior, 163
Lake Tangipahoa, Mississippi, 150–51
La Selva Beach, California, ix
law enforcement: counter-drug enforcement, 149; *long Island* Coast Guard cutter patrols, 32–33; paperwork for, 117; shift from SAR, 112–13; ticket quotas for, 114, 117
life rings, 7–8, 72, 131–32
life saving, 44
Lincoln Memorial, 147
Linnea (fishing boat), 96–101
Little League: coaching, 174; World Series, 179
Long Island (Coast Guard cutter): first tour on, 31; law enforcement patrols, 32–33; as miserable unit, 33; transfer from, 33–34; transfer to, 30
Los Angeles, California, 33, 149
loss, stories of, vii, 80, 84

Manresa State Beach, California, ix
Marine Corps, 25

maritime mall cop, 114
marriage: to D'Amelio, Courtney, 22, 27–28, 83; desires and limitations in, 30; long separations during, 27–29, 148
Marshall, Gene, 95, 99
Mayo Clinic recommendation, 187
Mecca night club, Kodiak, Alaska, 31
mechanics, 51, 128
medals: for acts of courage, 128; AFRAS gold, 145–46, 148, 153; to Chandler, 151; to Coast Guard Auxiliary, 150; commendation, 149; to Damico, 153–54
medical discharge: from New Orleans Station, 187; Nitrostat and, 188; vascular disorder and, 178
Merriman, Sarah, 111–12, 121
Mexico, 32, 33, 161
Meyers, Ross, 177–78
Midway Island, 26
Mineta, Norman, p5, 140, 149
missing persons reports, 87
Monterey, California, 28–29, 33, 34, 44
Mother Nature, 117
mourning, 84, 164
Murphy's Law, 100

National Motor Lifeboat School, 40–41, 44, 47
navigation skills, 4, 41, 176
New Orleans Saints, 147

New Orleans Station, p8; medical
   discharge from, 187; new
   position offer, 180–81; security
   patrols at, 179
Newport, Oregon, p3, 88, 120, 161,
   180, 182
newspaper interviews, 138, 140
New York, 148, 149
9/11 terrorist attacks, 60; fear in
   aftermath, 112; hysteria of,
   120; security patrols after, 113;
   US Coast Guard and, 111–14,
   149; void from,
   129
Nitrostat, 188
NOAA, 177
North Head Lighthouse, Cape
   Disappointment, 3–4, 6, 128,
   161
North Jetty, Columbia River, 4,
   39, 42, 106, 121, 129, 178;
   breakers at, 130
notoriety, 182
no-win situations, 11

Ocean Park, Washington, 4
Office of Boat Forces, 184
officer of the day (OOD), 111
omens, 125, 177
OOD. *See* officer of the day
operations officer, 125

Pacific Highway, California, 44
Pacific Sun (fishing boat), 65–71
Panama, 26
paperwork, 18, 85, 117, 125

patrol zones, 40
Peacock Spit, Columbia River:
   breakers at, 137, 152; capsized
   boat at, 121–22; check ride at,
   55–57; drowning at, 106–7;
   omen at, 125; shipwreck in, 77;
   view of, 39
Peacock Spit, high-profile capsized
   boat case: aftermath of,
   146; boat maneuvering for,
   130–31, 135–37, 152; crew for,
   128–29; drowning victim in,
   132–39; first visual in, 129–30;
   hypothetical questions for, 139;
   interviews for, 138, 140; media
   attention for, 145–46; rescue
   swimmer for, 131–32, 135,
   153–54; summary at awards
   ceremony, 152–53; survivors of,
   133–34; unwinding from, 141.
   See also Association for Rescue
   at Sea Award
USS *Peacock* (wreck), 77
Peter Iredale (wreck), 77
picnics, 154, 161
pilots: bar pilots, 41, 96–97, 118–
   19; boat pilots, 41, 79, 96;
   helicopter pilots, 9–11, 68–69,
   121, 128, 134–35, 137
Pittsburgh Steelers, 175
pleasure crafts, 3, 128
Pleasure Point, California, ix
Portland, Oregon, 117
powerlessness, 25
Pribilof Islands, Bering Sea, 19
pride, 25, 81164

punishment, 178, 180
Puzzle Palace, 125

quotas: for fishermen, 64, 163;
    ticket quotas, 114, 117

recession of 2007, 179–80
recognition, vii, 80; of heroism, 140
Recreational Boating Safety Patrol,
    3
regret, 73, 81
rescue swimmers, 140; for Peacock
    Spit high-profile capsized boat
    case, 131–32, 135, 153–54;
    reputation of, 135
retirement: house chores and
    child care in, 188; in Slidel,
    Louisiana, 179–80; vascular
    disorder and, 179
risk-taking reputation, 54
Ritvo, Ken: burn victim rescue and,
    77–80; as crewman, 95–96,
    98–99; naval background of,
    87; suicide victim retrieved by,
    88–89
rock management style, 182–83
rough surf, 6, 54, 183
running, 34–35, 44, 61, 91, 125, 146
Russian child drowning: brother's
    grief at, 12–13; distress call for,
    3–5; fear and, 165; guilt over,
    11, 164–65; helplessness at,
    9; red shoes and, 11, 13, 161,
    177; resuscitation efforts, 10;
    scene of, 6–8
Russian fur traders, 19

sacrifice, 30, 140
safety patrols, 3, 150, 161–62
Sanders, Mike, 54–57
San Diego, California, 33
San Francisco, California, 18, 22,
    116, 120
Santa Cruz, California, 28, 34, 44
SAR. *See* search-and-rescue
Sea King (fishing vessel), 80–81
search-and-rescue (SAR), xi;
    alarms, viii, 53, 61, 71, 82, 86,
    95, 121, 128; beatings from,
    66; in Bering Sea, 26; burn
    victim rescue, 77–79; calm
    in, 5; Camp Rilea helicopter
    crash, 81–83; at Cape D, 5, 34;
    discussions of, 82–83; do not
    become part of own case rule,
    133; fear in, 66; forchildren
    at Cape D, 3–13; guilt and
    regret in job, 73; in hostile
    weather, 5, 63; interest in, 26;
    life-and-death decisions in, 11,
    13; in mild weather, 3; no-win
    situations in, 11; over boat
    limitations, 64–65; praise for,
    150; shift to law enforcement,
    112–14; surfman in, 6; time
    for, 53; as vocation, 83; worst-
    case scenarios in, 97. *See also*
    capsized boats; disabled boats;
    drownings; Peacock Spit,
    high-profile capsized boat
    case; suicides
Seascape Golf Course, Santa Cruz,
    California, 28

security checks, 113, 117
security clearances, 179–80
security patrols: after 9/11 terrorist attacks, 113; at Cape D, 161; at New Orleans Station, 179
selflessness, 150
self-worth, 23, 164
Semper Paratus, USCG motto, 112
Sexton, Charles, 80–81
Sherman (Coast Guard cutter), 17, 20, 115; cleanup details, 112; first assigned to, 26; tours on, 29–31, 148; transfer from, 30
shipping containers, 118
shipping manifests, 118
shipwrecks, 45, 77, 80–81; lives lost and saved, 122
Siuslaw River Bar, p2, p4, p5, p6, p7; weather at, 182–83
Siuslaw Station, Florence, Oregon, 41; in charge at, 182; drowning at, 176–78; first house at, 171–72; master chief's rock management style, 181–82; move from, 179; routine at, 186; sale of house, 179–80; slap on wrist at, 185; surf training at, 183–85; transfer to, 3, 13, 161
Slidel, Louisiana, 179–80
slip tow, 98
Smithsonian, 147
smugglers: drug smuggling, 27, 32–33, 149, 179; weapon smuggling, 26
South America tour, 27

South Jetty, Colombia River, 4, 86, 126, 145
Statue of Liberty, 148
St. Paul Island, Bering Sea, 18–21
stress management, 83
stupidity, 44, 46
suicides, 88–91
superstition, 51, 58, 178
surf belts, 129, 131, 137
surfing, ix–x, 23; in Aptos, California, 41; childhood, 44; at A Jetty, 44–46, 85–87; ocean patterns in, 41–42
surfman, vii; absence from family, 121; achievement of, 5–6; Adkins as, 86–87; belief in value of, 73; breaking point for, 66; as dangerous job, 41; first big-wave case, 65–71; heavyweather surfmen, 40, 46, 126; intricacies of boat maneuvering, 135; knowledge needed for, 42; locations for, 6; Merriman as, 111; non textbook case for, 71–73; patrol zone of, 40; in search-and-rescue, 6; self-worth and, 164; surf training, p1, p2, p3, p4, p5, p6, p7, p8, 182–85; teaching of incoming and break-in, 54–56, 182–83, 185; temperament and demeanor for, 41; testing and qualifying for, 41, 47–48, 54; training for, 8, 40–41, 46–47, 135

surf zone, 43, 47; danger in, 55; ride
    into, 54–57; survival in, 56;
    tows out of, 63
survivors: from capsized boats, 122,
    138, 152; of Peacock Spit,
    high-profile capsized boat case,
    133–34; survivors' compartment,
    136; of *Tampa*, 151
Swain, Matt, 88–89, 118–19
swimming, 41

Tampa (freighter), 151
terror, vii, 71, 80, 151, 165
that guy at Cape Disappointment, 5
ticket quotas, 114, 117
Tillamook Head, Oregon, 4, 173
tows and escorts: at Cape D, 61–73;
    for large woman, 71–73; last
    tow, 161, 165–67; for *Pacific
    Sun*, 65–71; slip tow for, 98
Triumph motor lifeboat, 42, 51, 99,
    162
truck accident, 173–74

ugliness, 83
Umpqua River, p7, p8, 97, 182
Umpqua Station, Oregon, p7, 41,
    97; position offer from, 180
US Coast Guard (USCG):
    adrenaline surges in, 44, 61,
    95, 122, 140; boot camp,
    24–26; chief rank, 176; CISM,
    83; Coast Guard Auxiliary,
    83–85, 125, 150–51; coxswain
    rank, 41, 51, 61, 105; debts,
    financial obligations, and,

179–80; under Department
    of Homeland Security, 112,
    149; difficult for relationships,
    27; "do what's needed" as
    mantra, 57; dress uniform, 149;
    enlistment in, 23; evaluation
    of, 164; famed Sexton story
    in, 80–81; first joining, x, 5;
    isolated duty stations of, 19;
    maintenance of boats, 85; for
    maritime law enforcement,
    32–33; medical discharge from,
    178; 9/11 terrorist attacks
    and, 111–14, 149; operations
    officer, 125; ranking as Chief
    in, 13; respect for ocean, 3–4;
    responsibility in, 10; rule
    against leaving boat, 8; security
    clearances and, 179–80; *Semper
    Paratus* motto of, 112; small
    boat stations, vii–viii
US Department of Homeland
    Security: Collins and, 149;
    USCG under, 112
US Library of Congress, 147
US Treasury Department, 112

vascular disorder: diagnosis for,
    187–88; episodes from, 188;
    Mayo Clinic recommendation,
    187; medical discharge and,
    178; Nitrostat for, 188;
    retirement and, 179
Vietnam War, 26
violence, 83, 186
Vista, Martin, 27–28

Waikiki Beach, Cape
    Disappointment, 42, 84, 121
Wallace, Robert, 128, 136–37
Warren, John, 126–29, 131, 135–37
Washington, DC: assignments
    from, 186; letter arriving
    from, 146; orders from,
    112; sightseeing in, 146–47;
    wanting head on platter, 185
watchstanders, 51, 127; briefings
    from, 71; calls to and from, 4,
    39–40, 64, 67; training of, 83
Watkins, Jack: as Coast Guard
    Auxiliary, 83–85; death of,
    84–85; memory of dedication,
    85
weakness, 91; fear and, 164
weapons: Beretta handguns, 112;
    bombs, 90, 113, 118; weapon
    smuggling, 26
weather: in Alaska, 116, 147, 153;
    Bering Sea unpredictable,
    19; boats and, 42; Cape D
    constant change of, 117, 159;

Cape D extremes of, 51, 63;
    Columbia River Bar extremes
    of, 67–70; Columbia River
    Bar with temperamental,
    39–40; El Niño, 35; grating
    on nerves, 88; in heavy, viii;
    heavyweather surfmen, 40, 46,
    126; prediction of patterns, 66;
    SAR in hostile, 5, 63; SAR in
    mild, 3; at Siuslaw River Bar,
    182–83; waiting out storms,
    30–31
Wells, Jeff, 27–28, 44
White House: award ceremony at,
    147–49; sightseeing at, 147
Wisconsin, 163
work ethic, 24
World Trade Center, 148
worst-case scenarios, 97
wrecked vessels, 77

XO. *See* Executive Officer

Yaquina Bay, Newport, Oregon, p3